THE

CRY

OF

BEAUTY

By Hzal Anubewei

2nd Edition-Volume 2 (this volume contains revised books and new material)

Published by: OETRYHOUSE

PO BOX 217 Stone Mountain, Ga 30086

ISBN: **978-1-7346413-2-5**

Copyright: ©2021

hzalfaz@gmail.com

TABLE OF CONTENTS

The Cry of Beauty	7
The Cry of the Fathers	8
Evil: The Third Century	11
Natural Rhythms of Praise	12
No Flag	20
The Wall/ A Remembrance	22
The Commentaries– The War	24
Book of Atrocity: Octavia	28
The Ten Point Plan of Chicago	34
Ocmaba	38
Book of Two	76
Book of Order	78
Grease	80
The DO	84
The Lighted Rock	86
The Book of Now	88
Book of The Greyheads	90
The Union	93
The Winds of Change	95
Ocmaba: Book of Prayer	97
The Cycles: ARMAGEDDON	104
First Message	109
Travelling to the Word	111
Traffic	113
Day of Subtraction	115
Transfiguration	118
The Dead	120
The Empty Tomb	122
Horses With Eyes	128
Come	130
The Good Book	131

Zantioch	134
The Appeal	136
The Flame of HaHiYa	138
Revelations	142
Book of Thorns	143
Last Word	146
Fidance: Seal of Legat	148
Rise and Celebrate	150
Zero	152
The Book of Clarity	154
A Worker in the Field	165
The Suns Apple	178
The Book of Splendor	188

THE FOUR LIGHTS

From This Spot	202
The Book of Books	205
The Living Scripture	209
The Arc of Creation	212

Space is the soil of creation

Adapted from the original text of Seso. Also, includes writings by Octavia and Jake Motta. I have tried to place them in chronological order as best as can be determined. Other writings are from the Za'Koba's. This 2nd edition also contains the only video's of Seso : From This Spot, The Book of Books, The Living Scripture and The Arc of Creation taken from the archives and are the most complete presentation from that time. These four transcribed videos are also known as the Four Lights.

Seral

THE CRY OF BEAUTY

We
are the visitors of creation the witnesses of the body of the sun of diamonds of the green petals of the making of honey and so HaHiYa touched everything in creation with participation and each was given a season and creation was a garden for men of the worlds and magic to forever enjoy Participation in creation was of man's choosing and creation became a lliving language to inspire all men Our seeing one of feeling for the touch of HaHiYa is upon us all We witness the endless mystery the endless beauty of a natural form that works during our waking and sleeping hours moving always in harmony in complete steps through space into endlessness man could put away his tools his ships and his thoughts would not creation go on as silently as ever   would not the stars shine and the worlds fly in their orbits would not the waters run and the mountains raise themselves would not the air be bright and the plants roots as deep as ever and would not the weeping willow stand in prayer their brown and green limbs ever reaching out in praise of creation it is natural that we should mimic the creation it is so grand it speaks of the endless silence of wisdom of HaHiYa's great drama to inspire the worlds of men to be at peace to be silent and to know that

HaHiYa is with the creation always..... this is the Cry of Beauty

The

mind is imagination

the deep   let us divide the waters and fill it with creation that it might shine

be still

the Cry of Beauty is singing

this is endless

 endless

feel the silent magic

feel this endless warming glo....

    peace and peace and peace

THE CRY OF THE FATHERS

If
any man should ask let it be known that all of my activity is compelled by my fathers and mothers that lived before in all creation. That they are compelled by the father and mother of all things and thoughts.

If
I should go on a river and ask it for its name, it will say that through the ages it has always been water. And so, it is for all things of nature that are our companions. Water does not have a life of its own. None of us in creation have a life of our own but go together as if bound by a chord. Be not afraid for it is only the heart of He that has created life. It is male and female and all is compelled after HaHiYa I know that this creation is sweet. I have tasted it and I am blessed (at this time and now is forever, all the children of creation move and sing).

Dare
I change the ways of my father? My earthly fathers seem not to hear the Cry of Beauty of the water. They say it only ripples. They have found the things of their own hands more enchanting.

If
I should go on a mountain and know that height and the breadth and the weight then I shall know why men build cities. For the mountain is full of life. The mountain comes in styles and changes its dress in season. It relieves itself of all waste and allows for the balance of its populous. It lives a great life before it is done.

If
I should go to the animal world and speak with it, its voice will say it has not a will. I can never understand the fathers that hunt for prizes. The voice will say that it is its nature to eat that which was provided for it and nothing more. The voice will say it is not an experimenter but only a follower. The voice will say that there is a crying beckoning unto it so it goes.

If

I should go to a plant it will say that it grows from the earth, the air and sun. I have grown from my fathers. I have grown because of their life steps. The plant will say it does not have a history to learn from. It does not roam. That it breathes the world and serves the earth with its fruit. It lives for the feeling of the sun. This is a creeping affair ever reaching for some crying it feels.

If

we were allowed to visit the background of all things lliving in the creation we would witness the crying that silences in great sweeps of joy. It is the Cry of Beauty. It is but a child or so it seems. It is such a delight.

Dare

I change my ways. I know it is against the ideas and ways of the fathers before me and many in my company this hour. Our greatest books have been interpreted and written to give leadership to the fathers. That time is at end. The creator is male and female and envisioned the creation as such and thus it is. Everything lliving has its partner. All life is married. In my building past and present, and the building of the fathers, we mimicked the greatest design, the creation all around us and within us. The fathers as in other times no longer hear creation. They have become unfamiliar with its feelings therefore, the feel of life itself.

The

cities of the fathers do not support life abundantly. The buildings are rotten from the stench of minds inhabiting them. Our minds are in orbit of ourselves. The fathers have eaten a great measure of the treasure given the earth for hours of leisure. Nature has been covered up with the false material of technology and the disease of science fiction. The fathers have been made delirious by their handiwork. Love has gone out of the world. It has become a sad place. Admiration and truth look for a mouth out of which to speak. Many are now the villains in a world of tears. Let us grab this fallout and rinse it clean. The Cry of Beauty beckons me and I can hear no other sound none but the beauty of the silence.

Dare

I change the ways of the fathers that have disregarded the platform on which I now stand. My companions are losing their voice, too overcome with the smoke of the fathers to go on. Witness the natural things now false. The fathers and many others pretend to enjoy them. This is unnatural. The water choking. The animals corralled losing the language of their fathers. The plants, the trees fouled by the bad breath of the machinery of man. Darkness covers every road with the wildness of thieves and decay. The air sick with the waste of experiments. The earth appears strange to herself. She is so divided with nations crying for more.

HaHiYa

endows us with the freedom of manhood and womanhood. The earth is full with our companions and none here have been abandoned nor left to go astray. When the child hears the water he listens not to the ripple but to the song. The Cry of Beauty beckons us. We only have to quiet our heads.

EVIL: THE THIRD CENTURY

Are

not many of the old strikingly ill, no longer a film of health. Is not their life now in slow motion, then painfully dead still? And so, it is with the scene about us. The Third Century appeared in a blur. The bandit Science Fiction stands at the helm. Visit any city and notice how it hums, everywhere being given a new face, the image of health. The life held captive here painfully expanding through the days. The drama building is like a dull drumming until now the nervous system is smoking while the computers churn at data day and night at a blinding pace. All this to explain what the lawyer and doctor and politician and mechanic and the pilot and the governor and sanitation and hospitalization and insurance and Mercury 11 and revolutionist and what millions are saying. Even the specialists disagree as the categories overlap into one another. We are eaten alive in the expansion program meant to make life better, more lasting. Millions of willing servants tossed away into a world of nothingness. Look at the people with a three year old degree useless in the new world rearing its head. The mountains of the unfittable grows daily in search of a path that leads on. Once again, the wise ones are in serious search of the promised land.

And

so, you see Bandit is expensive. Cost us dearly. Surely the people have paid greatly to enslave themselves in this fashion. The banner of science fiction moves in a blue over the heads of the children. They will not have to wait for old age for grey hair. Their hungry hands reaching out to get a hold of this image before it disappears into the next year, offering their lives and their words in sacrifice before the flag of science fiction.

I

present to you the Cry of Beauty as a salvation. Take hold of its form and resurrect yourselves. Winter is at an end if you are among the willing. Learn to sing the new hymn, to change the air, wave Bandit goodbye no longer to entertain the thoughts of your mind. Let the wind of peace fill your being and sail into the afternoon of delights.

NATURAL RHYTHMS OF PRAISE

Possessed
of the dark skin born among the hirelings
we offspring cast off iron buckles
hundreds of thousands of voices call to us
from the bottom of the sea
speaking in tongues dead to us
we go to the islands
battle the battles of free men
the fires of sugar cane leap from the fields
men pretending to be mules turn in circles
women beside them
made to go naked in another man's house.
the birth of foreign babies
accepting this and more to go on.
hoodoo of voodoo lingering in the jungle
way past the morning
a thin line of drummers braving the new world to make music
knowing the passage of time will force a change
now another generation born
the bite of freedom the hand of a gun
a bit of glass
this people will be free
Haiti was born
file the documents for all of history to see
come to America
live among my brothers
the Cree, the Cherokee, the Blackfoot, the Sioux, the Apache, the Iroquois, the Algonquin tribes
the Amazon jungles of Brazil, the Incas
thousands of years before the Spanish landed in
converted canoes
follow our charts use our compass

those who were blackened long ago by moors
How did you forget the tribe that spawned Hannibal?
left your civilization for dead in barren hills
Khamit dying from old age
burdened by savages ignorant of the farmer
and his rules
so distant in time men no longer believed
yet among the bones of all men your scientist tell the
world we were already there before anybody else.
The dark past the truth hidden in our genes
so much like space we seem to be empty
come close and see this is a circle already full only needing
to find itself again.
the America's became the new breeding ground
to create us anew.
our strength kinky hair and adaptable genius
queen mothers
opening wide their legs releasing the latest product,
examined by cotton fields, broccoli, potato farmers,
railroad tracks, machines, the lash of a whip,
white women eyes and thighs
masters stiffness and our looseness
in a world of misery
cutting the air on sneaky nights with the ring shout
of Yoruba and Algonquin and Mali and Olmec and
chanting
calling out and responding
making the circle and creating anew,
at the gravesite marking with the old rituals
white folks afraid of dead folks sitting upright
walking the night with the ancestors
appearing at the crossroads with symbols
cigars knives and blood and pandemonium

calling on the powers of conjugation

making roots and giving new meaning to dead words

running for freedom under the cover of darkness

tricking masters and men for hire in broad daylight

facing the cruelty of white men separating mothers from daughters

the land charged with tears of fathers held down

at gunpoint

the rape of a civilization

uncorking the mile high attitude of a false religious race

greedily ran west   destroyed nation after nation

tying them under the noose of a word called Indian.

handing out paper documents

meaning to dispatch cavalries to slaughter innocents

at dawn

riding on trains with guns drawn mocking nature

intending to rid the land of buffalo, bear, wolf,

fox and beaver

the expense totaled to accountants

suppliers back east

high demand for flesh, animal and human

turning upon itself to right wrongs

fighting civil wars, Texas wars, Cuban wars, world wars

exiting into the modern world with guns drawn

the prototype of Rome with a flash

hip boots to wade in the reams of electricity

screaming long past nightfall

of a god given right to behave this way

the gifts of alcohol and heroin

boxer wars, Indochina wars, Korean, and Vietnamese and Iraqi

deadly wars against criminals making the news daily

sleight of hand tricks to intimidate the children of the

children of the children that your grandfathers raped and

worked

field hands skeletons studied by western scientist

puking at the knowledge

all these men worked too hard

their muscles ripped from their bones

grooves in their backs from the strain of too much labor

kaint see morning till kaint see night

kaint see morning till kaint see night

master on the verandah legs up on old nanny's back

where are the tears

where are the tears

watch my children taken at night sold at kristmas

given away during thanksgiving

those who look alike pointing fingers at those

of different colors: all you people look alike

say they are lazy, that they are thieves

that they are like children

living with an insane race of men

made the whole world sick

the disease of rats and roaches,

the black plague in Europe measles and strep throat

a race of men killing rivers and mountains

fighting over the right to kill as many trees as they like

the sickness of thinking

a drug of Plato a platter full of lies

removing everything that makes life simple

complicating everything

a boy genius on the earth clock barely a day old

denying everyone's history

coming with a flag and a book

to civilizations already suffering from decay

drawing his sword in the name of religion and other lies

behold this rider of the pale horse

Babylon at the door

painted with the bright red blood of a fresh kill

Khamit makes ready to rear her head again.

four generations of mating with herself

finding the root of her verb   springing into action

queen mother spreads open wide her massive legs

birthing new children

causing the spirit to rain upon her she multiplies herself

sending out the drum call

heard by her children spread all over the earth.

she speaks

at first eloquently in the voice of music

celebrating her new freedom

the jazz idiom rising from the ashes of pain

pushes all within its aura to new boundaries

raising the call of return to black

hit in the mouth by Douglas and Tubman

the selfcontained explosion of the Harlem renaissance,

the branches of this genius thought snuffed

out Rose a loft

a bus rider Rose through the ranks of time

shake America shake

to her knees

coming after Elijah, with Medgar , Malcolm and King

brown skin clouding the files of a Hoover

the helicopter flight of police to intercept this new breed

too late the thought was already out of the box

queen mother

busted another birth

unleashing the generations of warriors

fear gripped the white heart of America

fresh troops armed with drugs

technology posted a watch

to rid America of the Frankenstein she pimped

releasing a different energy

souls slipped into a deeper black

the drum of Khamit now lives within

to be to see myself as myself

rising into the atmosphere of a divine love

gathering hands to labor in the field of salvation

for the sake of the black nation

coming out on the other side

kinky hair flying

the sound of my voice more unique now than ever

Seso approaches the highlight film with words of his own

I am the Good Spirit

I am here for you all

get up black man

arise from the stupor of foreign elixirs

rise up from the South land

where your ancestors walked

pyramid builders mound builders

rise up from the concrete havens of the north

throw aside the dust and smog of the west

get to where you can see the witness of your God

HaHiYa

make noise from his heart.

make ready for his coming forth into the light of day

to claim our birthright

The branch of Khamit stretching its leaves bearing fruit

on the soil of America

step down now onto the earth

speak for the spirit of truth

know that salvation is at hand

the back of your servant is exposed

get up there

see the wonders unfold on the lap of creation

here a table fully laden with spoils of the victory

the roots of this seed laid in the Heb

seeking water in a far off land

get up black man for the water in the well draws near

called by the voice of one lifted on the wings of the cry of beauty

be not afraid

the clamor of the warriors' thunders on the ground

many step into alley ways

finding a descent that leads to back roads

fear has entered the heart of the masters

HaHiYa

has entered the fray

questioning his servant wisely

a council of souls strives against the mark

stricken with the tongue of falsehood

they pursue an evil way

the purpose of their destruction Seso

placed on a ship of peace

making his way town to town

to give a word of quiet

his mouth a cave overflowing with treasures

mothers and fathers greet him at the reception

celebrating with sweet meats and fruits of the vine

how much this servant suffers

the fingers of those who commit atrocities

locking away the children of bondage

making a place for them by the door where

they are to sit and wait until someone within calls

them by name

nonchalant about the day of salvation

passing them by

supposing that this holy one comes by name alone

guessing what the future holds

now black man get up
water is seeping while yet many are sleeping
others cry in despair and still more
claim the ancient law
doubt surrounds their heads and breast
men said he would send no more unknown to them
surely, they had a hand in making these arrangements
surely, they speak as one
meeting with the maker of plans
who would reach through time
throw open the gate
lead the children past thieves that hold them hostage
break the chains of bondage   open their eyes
the world seems strange to them
climb on the shoulders of the promised one
peep into the eye of tomorrow threw a curtain
witnessing the stars of glamour fall into the sea
see the unrighteous set upon by fierce lights
hold fast for the wind is high   moves with swiftness
clouds deposit stones of bitterness and cold
the heat is removed from bodies
even all those who have denied
the remnant of the children of faith
mercy rest upon their hands as they wrestle
hand to hand with the mighty of objection
the scroll of completion unfurls in the twilight
the battle goes down by Indiana and Ohio
served in a field where many are struck down
seek shelter none can be found to end this ruler ship
now get up black people
open wide your jaws and receive your enemies
praise HaHiYa
join the battle victory is yours as proclaimed

NO FLAG

The
Cry of Beauty is an invitation to your mind to review itself. Witness the stamina that entertains the worlds energy. The direction of human affairs. This offering revealed as the Cry of Beauty is simply the state of affairs as they appear on the screen of my mind to yours.

Creation
is such an endless gift. So, filled with love how can any portion deny this feeling. Love that colors nature so that it is most pleasing to the mortal eye. Water is flesh as we are yet it has not our ability to create nor has it the ability to distinguish between good and evil. It does not forbid access to its body. The rules of water are not written on her face. This offering is made by HaHiYa.

I
Seso offer unto as many as will receive the great message sustained by the Cry of Beauty. It says nature is speaking to you. It says the book of life that was intended for man has always been open to those who have the key. When the tree is talking open your eye and listen. When the water is in waves and moving and the whole moon is in the sky singing listen. When the winter has come and the sun has gone South and the dead leaves are buried by snows and the hairs of the animals grows thicker and many have gathered by the fire for warmth and the night has come for a longer stay women speak of the harvest that is in and the bear was seen going for hibernation then praise HaHiYa for in creation there is salvation as surely as the sun will fly to the North to revive the fallen. Without the shadow of a spoken word light bathes the world of our bodies and we hurry to pick the fruit nurtured under the heat. Hurry then to pick fruit brought to maturity by the light of the eternal thought that is guiding the orbit of fulfillment.

> I ask then no flags and rituals or cults
> I ask then no forms be made or symbols worn
> that men bow before

The
ways of the faithful cannot be lived within the confines of four walls for we all live in the world of the four elements and they are lesson enough for the wise and the ignorant.

I
ask that you who truly seek the hand of HaHiYa to take command of your thoughts and guide them into the orbit of love. There is much wisdom in the language of creation. Read the holy books for

surely the allegorical prophets speak a sublime truth. Therefore, seek not to raise a banner in praise of any earthly thing but seek the truth for it alone remains untouched through eternity.

The life revealed by my words is merely one tree that has seed in the earth and grown roots. There are many trees that have taken root and there are many yet to come. Before them I am humbled as I am before all creation. Go your way after having read these words and take with you what you love and then look further. Revelation in creation is endless and there are other trees preparing to take flight.

...the root of HaHiYa is endless..........

THE WALL

The nature of Seso was a sweet meat, actions the petition of his words. It was this that caused the more undisciplined nature of many to react violently to the presence of Seso. Let the reader be advised how often a field of good yield is plundered by ignorance and greed. Set upon by the mob of darkness.

The
material for the Book of Atrocities was provided by eyewitness accounts, articles by Don Lake, a news reporter assigned to follow the activities of Seso; from notes and letters of Octavia and a special section composed by Jake Motta. The material was adapted by the Unknown Writer and came into the publishers hand as found here. The dialogue throughout is a living testament to the spirit of Seso and another stone lodged in the grand gate of the spirit of creation. Other than through rumor this description given here is the first written testament concerning the gate or long wall of praise that Seso was claimed to have spoken of only on rare occasions. The text is evidently not complete but we are certain that the reader of this book will gain new insights into Seso.

peace and peace and peace

A REMEMBRANCE:
(from the unknown writer)

I was standing a way off when Seso first began speaking. A small group of us had met in the living room of Jake. This was maybe the tenth time I'd ever been in the company of Seso. I didn't think to write it down. In fact it wasn't until about four or five years later that I thought on it again. Not until I saw Seso outside of Chicago. He was pretty well known by then and I had left his little band back in Indianapolis for a job in Chicago. Well, when I saw him and Jake it all came back. I don't remember it all but here is what I recall Seso saying:

In a place of somewhere there exists a long wall composed of the faces of all the prophets of creation. Angels without number sing in endless praise of their works and announce their revelations. Wise men of the lower worlds hear and the heavens hear their chanting. The wall is like a silvery mist and horses with long purple fire manes and flaming eyes prance all about. Flowers of endless descriptions appear and give their perfume. The sound of a deep humming moves. The faces are the faces of those old and new, those yet to come. And in the midst the great tree that spits fruit existing before the beginning of time..

I saw this in my mind that day before Seso spoke a word and was unable to utter a sound.

THE COMMENTARIES
(taken from a book written by Jake Motta)

As
we sat on the bottom of the Rocky Mountains of Colorado my thoughts repeatedly returned to the refugees of California lost in Denver and other cities. It was similar to every scene in every city of any size in the country. People divided by money and color. It was my association with the breeze of Seso and my subsequent travels in the world that caused my thoughts to become at peace. That time hadn't come completely yet. I admit not only to being confused but to anger as well. Undirected anger at men in general. We seemed to be so weak. WE didn't believe.

The
thoughts raced through my mind that day. How long has man suffered? Why was it that generation after generation of men from many tribes heeded not the warnings before them? Merciful HaHiYa, we have heated ourselves and the prophets and messengers sorely. A generation should be born in tears and live a century without uttering a word and pass away. Let this be a sign to men of the endless glory of HaHiYa. Yet, as before, as now, men live that see not the great blessings, praising themselves until the end of their days.

When
I told Seso my thoughts he spoke the following words. Of the conversations we had this one is very close to my thoughts and heart. Seldom does a day pass that I do not reflect upon it. I have collected what Seso said that day and called it The War.

THE WAR

?When my grandmother Alul passed from this world I wept, not for her, for her passing to that world was joyous. My tears were for those who lived and believed in the world of appearances.

O
man has suffered a long and ceaseless time. Having twisted himself, his family and his nations into knots, he then falls into dismay, drawing generations into the darkness with him.

It
is by design that the worm passes the earth through his body and his life is complete because it is the way for him. Man hears not the sound of its crunching, the cycle of toil, of struggle beneath our weary feet. By what name do we call the many wars of existence? The seed that must fight its

way to the light struggling for room to grow, to branch out. A tireless battle goes on. Man does not hear the battle but is a witness to the fruit. What a lovely flower. What sweet melons. Man, alone introduces treachery to the battle, doing so because of the illusion of loss. By his influence life is being washed ashore lifeless. It is a battle without purpose. without cause. It is the nature of this world to change, to struggle, to weed itself and the world proceeds daily without excess.

Grandma Alul

was a warrior. She was a child of the fifth house coming to life in flames. She spoke of herself as a soldier. Those of you who remember her, did you witness the mountain on which her soul took refuge while the earth besieged her on every side with naked men and women, liars and magicians, poverty and storms. She passed her years immovable from the mountain where she looked down on the rains below.

In

this world are armies and all the people here are soldiers. Let not the idle imagine that their hours are passing leisurely. Is not their game gathering alone or in-groups at some enchanted spot boasting of their cleverness while young and leaving no one in tears when their time is done. What this army has not taken upon itself is responsibility and are not they their brother's keeper?

I

have taken root in the earth for my history. My thoughts are leaves turned toward the light. As the soldier of love, I go about among the people to feed myself. There are those who called my walk through the America's wandering. My feet are free. The spirit of HaHiYa guides me where he will. Are not the lives of men regimented or are there those who lay claim to a creation of their own?

Nothing

is ever lost in this garden. Not the drunk, not the bum, not the rich, not the pregnant nun. Man did not invent the creation or its laws, nor did he set it spinning. Let us be wise and admit that most soldiers have no desire to lead. They desire to spend their time in this world casually. The greatest soldier is he who is the servant of all men for he is a foundation. It is drama for the minds of men and must appear over and over so that men know that it is truth.

I

Seso, have come to this world as an example. Come before men of the world with my words and actions to show man that the Sun of glory is ever shining and that the world is not consumed in darkness as some have supposed. Men know that the earth revolves on its axis causing day and night. It is the same with the spirit of man. One moment we can see the light, the next moment there is darkness. We go blank in the heat of daily battle to survival. We do not think that ignorance guides us into falsehoods. In truth, the light remains with us always. It is we who are revolving. We must learn to keep the light in our eye like the moon. Creation speaks to us daily if we would but listen.

The
Cry of Beauty is the light of the word of Creation. It has come to remind us that the war we are fighting was won with the first story of creation when man began as the spark of HaHiYa. The light of wisdom llives. Put away the thoughts given us. Let us stop this spinning away from the Light. By the mercy of HaHiYa was this creation given as a sign to man so that his stay here would not be a long walk in darkness. The light fills the path of the prophet and his soldiers. They are neither revolving nor straying but give their eye wholly to what is before them. Their faces appear like the new moon to the observers of a more earthly life.

Turn
not a stone away. Keep the tempo and march on. The Cry of Beauty is the first wind. Let it surround you. Breathe it deeply. BE a witness. DO perform in this drama. Feel yourself glo..

~~~~~~~ ~~~~~~~

Seso
throughout his life was such an endless channel. So much of the good came through him. I have begun this recapitulation concerning Seso with The War because this was what the whole drama was about. The world at large witnessed what they believed at one point to be an ideological struggle, later an economic struggle, finally a political struggle with overtones of a united revolutionary front spearheaded by Seso?? The believers of men were once again in error. Seso's war was with the image of life as men of power were driving it. Oh, my people can you yourself not see the why? Is not life drama? Is not creation a tireless picture that gives birth to itself?

 Seso
was a witness to the beauty of this and the beautiful stories it gives helps guide a seeker deeper and deeper into the realms of wisdom. When Seso spoke to the ears of men it was a proclamation for their thoughts were holding dead images. Creation had become a laboratory for their little magic to whip up one miracle product after another. The image they gave to the world was science fiction, proclaiming it as salvation for man.

The
war was a war of images, the real, which is lasting and the unreal, which is self-destructing and full of glitter.

There is only one creation and this is the creation that Seso loved. The words of man but copies. Who gives these copies praise and the label of immortality? By what name can man conjure up to call the figure of atrocity entertained and beheaded in the face of the messengers of HaHiYa's sweet flowers?

Have
they forsaken the original creation for one of their own? What of those who create nothing by their hands or imagination except ignorance and entrapment for themselves and their whores? Are they not more kin to the vipers that slither on their bellies to hypnotize their prey, feeding forever on others?

O
blinded seekers of joy would HaHiYa increase the breeze of Seso tenfold you would call it an unusual tempest and struggle that much harder for you have hardened yourselves supposing that you are impregnable stones.

We
watch your collisions in the hells you have created. You are the stones that sink not in the waters but are tossed about wildly in each new wave. We are the flowers of the earth gathered before the face of HaHiYa that sink deeper in the waters than you hard stones...

excerpt from writings of Jake Motta

--the woman that travels with Seso, a former scholar, that gave up a promising career made an abrupt departure ten years ago to join the Seso movement. A native of? Cleveland, she rose from the depths of poverty to world prominence. A gifted student of biological research, and beautiful, her attachment, to this writer, has at times seemed farfetched. The space flowing out of the Seso movement has bewildered many. Perhaps the true Octavia, the poor fatherless child reared in the ghetto, is showing her true color!

—-don lake

The
above vicious and unconscionable article was written by Don Lake, a flunky for Dakk Runn and big business in general. This article came out seven years prior to the capture and unlawful holding of Seso and Octavia at the palace of Dakk. Through men like Don Lake, Mr. Runn directed a successful campaign against Seso. It was successful because of the bigotry that refused to accept the message of a black man. Beginning as he did in Cleveland, dubbed the mistake on the lake the same signature was drafted on to him. Anyone who ever felt the breath of the Creator could not deny that man and woman, Seso and Octavia, and those who followed closely at their heels were in touch with something very powerful and sweet, something holy. I could look into their eyes, listen to their words and be filled.

The
following concerns a comment written by Octavia that I was given by her. The major portions of which I lost on the TRAIL OF TEARS. The journey after the quake was arduous with so many confused by their new life and the devastation that brought it into reality. May you read and understand the greatness of the last few years. Peace to you Seso and Octavia and Jake and Yasoon..

--the unknown writer

OCTAVIA SPEAKS

His form was lliving peace. His hands moved effortlessly like a petal in the winds. I would look in his eyes and it was like gazing at the stars or like falling. I loved Seso because he was complete. I felt only sorrow for those who did not understand. And I felt anger at those who injured him physically and emotionally. I understood that they were driven by precious traditions and men who thought for them. Still I felt anger. I prayed and Seso would say do not be angry. What they do they feel in their hearts that they are as right we are. He would say that our work was to remind them about the truth in this time. That it would take time for words to enter their consciousness and take root. He would say right actions would bring many into the fold quickly but men needed the lliving word to speak to their souls for them to continue.

I remember men and women who had never seen us before cursing us foully. When we first began in Cleveland, Seso would go to a lagoon in front of the art museum in what was called University Circle. It was a good setting. Saturdays and Sundays and even weekdays, snow or rain or sunshine we were there. It began to take hold. Poets and musicians and people all there listening to the message of Seso.

On one occasion, a man who had given up a criminal life, came throughout the winter and in the early months of spring gave himself to follow Seso. His name is Jake Motta, a big fierce looking man. I remember his words as if he spoke them today. I've been listening to your words for six months and I have watched the many different faces that have appeared and disappeared and have seen the drunken saying amen. I observed you three Wednesdays ago when four ministers questioned you on your meaning. I heard you speak of the Cry of Beauty and that you called God HaHiYa, the Hand of Life. It was made clear to me that the mind is a tool of the lower world and like Cain was a hunter of things or your commentary on the end of Pentecost, forty-nine days according to the legend ascending on the first day of the week, a celebration of Kaniya and making H'ristos a house of Thoth. And what of Simon Kepha as Petros in Rome holding the fish of Vishnu, or Icthus; blood Appolonius, of Chrestos and Eros; the ministers left to ponder these things. Never in my life have I seen such a man as you. The strength of the eternal tree is lined in your voice dropping words whose symbols have bottomless fathoms to delve in. Never have I heard the language of our people lifted so high pouring forth like a fountain.

From the day Jake joined us the light ascended in his eye and forehead. We would listen for hours as Seso unfolded his thoughts for us and we saw a creation we never saw before.

O

HaHiYa what strength you gave us. The day is clear in my mind when the police came to us at the Heb with a legal complaint of corrupting the minds of the community and especially children with inflammatory statements and revolutionary activities. Those who worked against us did so because of our color and because our words, Seso's words, gave the world a new look. He dared to reject the words of the fathers of this world. Rejected their god, their traditions, their everyday ways and beliefs. Seso meant change and a true turning point in the black man's history and was a beginning and ending unto himself and the merciful HaHiYa had created him in this manner for the work he so willingly cultivated until it took root.

Cruelty

during this time had become a first cousin to us. It has lain in wait for us at our door or wherever we have gone. At first, I was in constant fear for my life. My heart felt as though it had shrunken to the size of a peanut so tried we were. Seso quietly and patiently said to me, be strong. HaHiYa is with us and will soon remove this burden form our hearts and minds. I can't tell you in words the transformation the growth, the stillness that eased into my heart and soul. It was as if the world was coming to a halt or the calming of deep water. No swells only deep still water. I entered myself becoming a witness to the rock understanding what Seso meant by the lighted rock. I was no longer in the midst of things. I walked in the Light of day. They will not believe that from that moment the blows we received to the head and heart only glanced off this shiny armor. I could smile within myself and be still and know that what they did they did out of fear. I have kept a journal of these things along with papers of Seso's in THE WALK THROUGH THE AMERICA'S.

The

days when we first left Cleveland there were only seventeen of us. It was in the spring when we left on foot. We were branded as fools. What did we hope to gain by wandering about the countryside, here and there without a plan or destination? Who did we think we were? Wasn't it written that no prophets were to come? Wasn't it written about the son? What madness was this?

We

asked them about the Bab and Baha'u'llah and Martin and Elijah? Were not these men messengers? Are not all men brought into the world (or sent) to sing the praises of the Creator and do his work, resurrecting ourselves from the death of ignorance and rise into the heaven of revelation? I know not others meaning neither actions or their words. I am aware of my obligation and condition. I see my people and listen to their suffering. Am I to be still with wisdom and vision? I have felt the breeze of Seso. I have considered his words and actions.

I have been lifted up spiritually into other worlds, receiving the prayers and good will of citizens of Plictah and women long gone from this plane of events. Always, always it has been the same: HaHiYa invented the creation and thus it is so. Will you not love that which is grander than yourself, who has not left you in darkness but put light in the way, forever and ever. I go spinning daily and it is the holiest orbit for HaHiYa's hand is guiding me.

Those that questioned so severely about our destination were living for the image overshadowing their lives. America and the American way. Exclusive not inclusive. Words and slogans rotten in the mind and hearts while children went begging in the world, living in filth and ignorance and dreaming or scheming a way out of misery. They were afraid because adventure had gone out of the world. Man and woman had become the standards of behavior, predictable time clocks. Taking the abuse of men and phony laws invented by men to protect their wealth. Creating separate governments within false national boundaries.

Slaves at each other throats fighting over crumbs thrown down from the darkening clouds of power. I took Seso by the hand and said: Let us go into the wilderness of the new square of forty degrees and if we should die then let it be by the hands of nature, whose skin is real, rather than by the hands of that which is lifeless and faithless. My name is love, let them kill me if they can. In the name of HaHiYa by His mercy, lay out His words for all to see. I go to do this work. If by chance should I fall then I will have died for the work of creation and not by the cause of man who does not know the way.

The children of darkness have fallen on us every day. Taking every opportunity to plunder this sweet garden. They have sought to pluck our eyes and minds. They have enticed us by every manner imaginable, using every tool at their disposal to enslave us, bring us back into the fold. We have seen their corral and reject it. We have rejected the novelty and fame of the video and the printed word. They have taken us prisoner in their jails and wronged us. So great has the madness been they brought us naked into the street for ridicule and placed thorny wreaths on our heads. On a plain outside Chicago, we were charged with inciting a riot that led to the death of over five hundred innocent souls. We were thrown in jail and given poison for refreshment. We have died a thousand deaths, been burned, and bitten and I in my heart can say, HaHiYa invented this creation thus it is so. It is His hand that has guided me and I am assured of an abiding peace.

It was strange at first residing under the stars, waking in the morning and knowing on the morrow we would awaken in another place. Every day nature starred for us revealing her secrets of herbs and other good things to eat. We lived with Indians in Arizona in the desert and mountains eating what they ate and listening to their stories of ancestors from the old men and women, learning about the Great Spirit. Not once did Seso attempt to give them HaHiYa as a substitute but listened gladly as I did. When he spoke, it was like a gentle warm hand extended in friendship and understanding. They knew HaHiYa.

We went all over the country and Seso was asked to talk or read his poetry and everywhere we were threatened. The name of Seso passed along by rustlers and cowards. The media making us more and more visible. A glamour market developed through t-shirts and other paraphernalia. Funds funneled into the Heb, all marketed legally in the name of Seso. The work of the media to confuse what Seso was about worked. The name had been co-opted. Seso knew then he needed to disappear for several years and he did.

It was true that Seso called god HaHiYa, that he wrote a book called the Cry of Beauty and that he sought to change the image of the world of things. But Seso never claimed to be a prophet nor did he ever have any army of five thousand trained guerrillas. It was a plan by the powers to wreck the greatest gathering of Abukan Americans, Abukans, Hispanic, Asian and other third world countries. The mulatto children of many nations ruled or conquered born into this world not knowing who they really are. The black children of Abukan descent living in the so-called new world before the days of Columbus. The people of the Mayans and Toltec's and other tribes of so-called Indians already indebted to the children of Nubia for science and religion. The children of ancient Khamit. Nubian descendants of Ethiopian lands and others, tracing themselves back through ancestors that raised children on the continents of Lemuria and Atlantis before North became South. Seso lifted the veil on the seven churches breaking the seal of secrecy held there. Chasing away the demons of falsehood, shining a bright light on lies and misfortune. The Ten Point Plan of Chicago was the end result of a week of co-operation and love and the resolution was planned for adoption the next day. That night police moved in claiming they had news of a riot and gunshots were fired. The great step ended in blood.

Our
last place of work before we were forcibly held was South America. Many of the people there are still close to the earth and listened well to the words of Seso and he to theirs. A shaman of Mexico met us in Yucatan and we journeyed into the sacred mountain place of the Andes in Peru. Spiritual power was met there and a cleansing of the way was made.

Octavia,
peace and peace and peace

THE TEN POINT PLAN OF CHICAGO

(this document comes to us only as a fragment destroyed
in the attack of the police. also included is a very short list
of participants as well as some dialogue from Half Eagle,
who recalled these events for us this day)

-the unknown writer-

The
economic situation of the country was deplorable. The third quarter report affected us greatly as funds for the Indians Nations were drastically cut for the third straight year. Federal cutbacks and state aid programs all suffered. The Middle East was in flames again as voters sought to roll back guaranteed funds for the state of Israel. Civil war raged again in Mexico and Peru, South Abukan and tensions between France and Italy were deepening. The U.S. suffered through the second straight year of violent civil uprising in its major cities, particularly Dallas where the Mexican American population had it with no political voice. Blacks and Latin Americans and Orientals had banded together in Orlando, Chicago, New York, Philadelphia, and the West Coast. It was indeed a dramatic background. The most powerful disruption however came from the Asian community as its diverse groups banded together as a result of their prominence on the world scene.

Obviously
there was much dissent initially as these extremely diverse groups sought to come together under one umbrella. The actual committee work lasted nearly two weeks as the language and concessions were pounded out until a general consensus was garnered. Many participants walked out in disgust leaving behind only a working crew. However, the patience and driving energy of Seso, all agreed, bore fruit and the resolution, fragile as it was, was adopted with the next meeting ten years in the future. Immediately upon accepting the initial draft groups began to meet to jockey for positions of power and control. The framework was laid. The ten points have been lost due to the destructive forces at work both within and without the council. It is sad that the deaths of so many who had worked so hard stymied the completion of the final draft. My name is Half Eagle and the day we were so treacherously attacked is a day of infamy. I looked at my brother Seso and pointed to my tongue: they came to my people, to my ancestors and we stretched out our hand to them, the hand of friendship and love. The years passed and we saw not only our destruction but watched as the whole world was broken by their benevolence. They speak with fork tongues, forked tongues. I will not let the words of these men die on the ground where they lie but will gather them

to my bosom and carry them to those who despised them and throw them in their face. I will wage war forever. I saw my brother Seso shed tears that day for the sadness touched us all. Many of us took to our knees. Seso asked for forgiveness. It was the day of sadness and was included in THE TRAIL OF TEARS written by Seso--- Half Eagle

-it was agreed the word TRIBE(s) would be used to identify the various groups and also because of the words significance in reference to unity and one mindedness. Seso pointed out that in this country the word had been erroneously given an historical or primitive connotation, when in fact the nations of Indians were united under a treaty and were in fact the original United States as described by the Algonquin Nations. It is more correct to understand that all men belong to a tribe and are descendants of such and that the present confusion exists as a result of trickery and prejudicial men that seek to twist the meaning of words.

RESOLUTION 1) a u*:

We the Tribe (s))), herein agree and adopt binding ourselves and our partners, the following resolution (s)) and placed it first in all matters of human and spiritual conduct wherever we find ourselves and our fellows. The matter herein pertaining to the presentation of ourselves as having inalienable rights given by the Creator in all matters concerning rights regarding seeking first our God above and beyond all other considerations.

Without the Creator all is lost.

*agreed upon (a.u).)

RESOLUTION 2) a u:

concerning our freedom of speech; the right to speak freely at all meetings public and private

RESOLUTION 3) a u:

The recognition of the Constitution as the law governing our earthly conduct one with another and among the various nations.

RESOLUTION 4) a u:

Ownership of property unencumbered against all past present or future loss and the filing of documents to insure the same

RESOLUTION 5) a u:

    Each man and woman pursuing the highest goal attainable according to their particular skill and qualification without limitation

RESOLUTION 6) a u:

    The treatment of one another according to what is right without question or prejudice

RESOLUTION 7) a u:

    The provision of funds relative to health and welfare in times of need. An allocation of five percent of all revenue gathered by the tribes.

RESOLUTION 8) a u:

    The establishment of a general fund placed under an oversight committee to gather monies for a period of not less than five years of continuous contributions at a rate not to exceed three percent of revenue per nation or group participating as one of the founding tribes and their subordinates.

RESOLUTION 9) a u:

    Vow never to knowingly injure, make war, deceive or anyway cause wrong to befall one another, seeking always the way of peace and harmony, remembering that the Creator endowed all with the right to pursue the right to life and happiness without injury as regards economics, culture, and religious pursuit, marriage, and destiny of person without personal injury or insult, or disadvantage

RESOLUTION 10)a u:

    The equality of men and women in all pursuits in accordance with inalienable rights endowed by the creator and bestowed as a right of life, respecting the sovereignty of each individual

It is to be understood that this document is not to be misconstrued as a vehicle of containment but rather as source of inspiration and celebration of human achievement.

The separate stairs on the spiral merge here as both material and spiritual conduct reflect unity as the base or root of the Tribes.

the day walks near when the rhythm of my
people shall be the means by which they
untie themselves from the hard knot of oppression
setting for themselves an orbit no man can pass by.
They will have no more fear of themselves and will
be feared among all men
HaHiYa speaks for the black man
their hands clean
their thoughts repeating HaHiYa's
solemn oath:
The
earth is full of calamity
will you not cease
the law is tireless
while the criminal soon is weary of the chase
Join all you hand to hand
consider the earth a virgin place
as innocent as you regard your brick temples
Say
the earth is as holy as heaven
imagine that love is ever present
that I grow daily to become the lighted rock
I will pass the gate
share witness with all in my presence
none are a stranger to me
Our orbits are but fleeting circles
surely we are flying home
surely we are flying home...

OCMABA

The word of HaHiYa is unfailing

join with it and go forth into that which was previously unknown

        OCMABA (the act of becoming knowing)

When you can view that which is out of view and have come to know the ninety points of the Ocmaba then it will be said of that one he truly knows the way of peace.....

The acceptance of the pathway to HaHiYa comes from within where the seed takes root. This acceptance is a dawning reality of the knowing becoming or the Cry of Beauty, Ocmaba is the pathway. Those aspects of life are reflected in the natural things around us. View the heavens and witness the rising and setting suns. A voluminous light the day and bright speckles and moons shining in the night sea. A simple concept of HaHiYa that never is any part of creation in darkness. The knowing becoming of that witness among all things. (1st degree)

we accept HaHiYa as the creator of creation

we accept the laws governing life

we accept that life has a purpose to become

we accept the responsibility to know right from wrong

we accept joy and misery as arms on the same body

we accept the differences among men therefore we all require patience

we accept that peace is unstable and we must strive to protect it

we accept that no man or government is greater that God permitting ourselves to acted upon as if we were animals

we accept submission to HaHiYa's glory and mercy and grace

we accept faith as a step in consciousness and knowing more than believing

we accept knowledge is a step to wisdom and wisdom is a step to becoming

we accept the coming one in each and every capacity of life

These are some of the degrees of the Ocmaba. Recipients prepare your vessels to receive these beginnings. Is not the body your sacred temple nurtured by plants and fruits and liquids. Know the aspects of what is good and warm and even more. Acceptance is application. Viewing that which is out of view.

Travel if you will into the breath and become its witness and it will unfold its light for you. All life has moments of pause and moments of activity. Will you not cease and be still and quit your endless rambling of body mind and spirit? Peace will not come until there is silence. Viewing that which is out of view.

The
seamless fabric of creation falls not apart at any point, recreating itself at ANY POINT. Know that when HaHiYa made this portion he made others in places out of view each no less wonderful. If we were there we would consider ourselves alone when nothing that can be seen here was created by itself to be alone?
The
Ocmaba considers that which can be seen felt or touched or heard or smelled or thought and those things which are beyond, go about their business without man's awareness beyond the hand of man.

GREETINGS

    this is the first day
    except for HaHiYa
    all things have a beginning
        the point of entry a celebration
    birth is the key word
    set upon its new journey
        like all babes the light wanes here
    it will take three times the path of
        the moon
    to reach the land where the sun
        waits to cross
    there if you are patient awaits a key
        to unlock
    the golden treasure

INTO THIS WORLD

we go as those with their hand over
    their eyes
crawling on our hands and knees
a mother waits upon us
young and lovely, the cycle revolves
    endlessly
how can we stand when we are yet so
    new
a suckling babe at the breast of life
the milk still sweet in our mouths
what do we know of life
having suffered none of the pain of it
our faith and trust and security lie in
    the hands of others
behold yourself in the mirror of life
helpless even to feed or wipe your
    own spoiled cloth

FIRST WORDS

the animal in me is now apparent
the teeth in my mouth separate me from
all other creatures
my stomach prepares to receive the food
I
place in my mouth
the moments of my fledgling individuality
    has begun
the undertaking I have prepared myself

        for rears its opposite heads
the steps I take set me upon this path
  once begun they can never be retraced
  they are now only memories

ORBIT

the cycle is like a spiral
traveling faster and faster
the wheel moving exponentially
the long legs of a runner armed
with the books of the ages
children of spring full of color
the songs of planting fill the air
feeding on the early rains and
rising sun

pray that the moon's eye fades not
this being the third time they have
        looked
nor that the beetles and things multiply
so fast they overtake the young seedlings

THE RED STAR

a traveler full of fire
marshaling the forces of nature
release the inner energy or toil in vain
go to the market place
a man waits there for you with a calming tea
small sips by the bed at nite
quiet thoughts and slow breaths

the next day is yours
within yourself know the battle has been
       won
your station looks like victory
don't forget that there is more to do

LOVELY WOMAN

the face is the mask that changes
on the same head
when we returned the child was now
       a young woman
perhaps there is more to the dance
       than just music
alluring eyes can be as deadly as
       kicking feet

if by chance the night is not over
then glance at her through the eye
       of a halfmoon
fleeing toward the horizon before
       the master of the house comes home

FRIENDS

there we were at a graduation together
making plans at the future table
the distant crying of children seeming
       to warn us
our happiness closed our eyes and ears

gold turned to silver then to brass
now it is not a metal at all

what we see is not what we saw then

it is funny that I share wine with another
who stood somewhere off stage
quietly we always cheered for one another
now we talk as never before

TIMING

you should not be here
I was just going out the door
it was my turn to lead the parade

everybody is driving too slow
late to work late paying the bills
lent money to my uncle
now the hot water tank busted
got two feet of water all over the floor

sometimes it doesn't matter when
     we get up
things are going to happen
don't get so bent out of shape
relax laugh let it go

CROSSROADS

the master of the house is coming home
a king upon his throne
seed the ground the sky throws rain
all eyes move to the heavens
move across the hemisphere prosperously

cutting off the heads of those who oppose
      him
announcing a celebration he orders all in
      the realm to attend
feed them richly drink the finest of wine
suddenly the ass's colt bolts untethered
the kings rides upon him
guest mock him knock him to the ground
ten maids in attendance see to his wounds
      he is weaker than before

if you would be king and master then listen
tell a true story of heavenly majesty
      the moons silence for three nights
all rise together very early to celebrate
one forty three the end of the mystery
      bones do not rise alone

MYSTERY

Man
is not the mystery
HaHiYa
is the mystery
Men think that numbers came alone
Men count lights in the sky
circling and extinguishing themselves
HaHiYa
is the mystery
Beginning the day of days work
Placing a wind between atoms
friction in space

No man knows the day Space began
No man knows the atoms aroused
each thing taking form
East and West a square
North and South the triangle
time spun away
HaHiYa the hand of life
choose love as the pole of action
Gave the created a face
moving from an original place
never to return
the eternal exodus of the prodigal son
HaHiYa
is the mystery
boneless   seamless
without a single breath of life
space supports the door of the living
where atoms gather to express wisdom
showing themselves as planets and stars
dead animals lying on their face
silently absorbing the music of the heavenly wind
turning burning suns without touching
never lost in space
men look upon all that can be seen or heard or felt
wonder how all this came to be
chasing magic to duplicate creation
HaHiYa
is the mystery
not men who try to count the uncountable
spinning in space

I

I
have made a path of my own
I take that which is square and make it round
the journey of my life is on my hands
a special decree granted by HaHiYa
a gift to be used
worry not to detractors
stay the course
Uranus has marked the place where you churn
milk into butter

think not that a man is an island
vanity creeps like a vine
a strange thing winding itself among the trees
looking down on you spinning in dirt

DARK CLOUDS

A
thousand voices murmur in the water
dark clouds rush in low to the ground
the deep comes down to earth
in these moments cling to the heart of HaHiYa
severe lessons prepare themselves
nipping at the heels of the unsuspected

remember that above the ground above the dark clouds
stars are burning brightly day and night
never is a man without a visible path to walk upon

SIXES & EIGHTS

u & n   w & m   d & b
similar
asymmetrical
seeing others in myself
knowing where I stand
no need to ask questions
my own grade a finger pointing
a long tongue wagging uselessly
every dog has his own bone

sometimes it is better to spend a day at the beach
look into water listen to the waves
a day when the mouth should do nothing but be quiet

MUMBLE JUMBLE

A
muddled situation
a collapsed star
desperate and confused
imagine a monk running amok
wine spilling from the hand of a paralyzed man

take time to recycle the world around you
study the fourteen days of the moon
dig deeper into your dreams
avoid the criminal element or meet the fate of Osiris

THE ATHLETE

they
come faster than time
increasing the rhythm around them
pushing the human boundary to a new limit
the elements of electric impulses speed through
the brain
kinetic energy explodes jacking muscles to perform
athlete lift up your eyes and be grateful
  be thankful
gifts chose their recipients wisely
HaHiYa chose you
those who lead be careful of what others might see
Samson gave away his hair
place not your hands on the enemy's temple
bringing down the world with you

TUSSLE

A
man fought with me through the night
morning came with the peace of the rising sun
when
we think our hands are tied
some take the time to throw stones
we
gather our weaknesses in a basket to go to market
trying to sell ourselves cheaply
thinking this only happens to me
a mad thought not being ourselves

speak when you awaken to others
it happened to you too
step down from this pedestal
step up from that hole you made to cover yourself

the man you fought with through the night
only comes to others during the day

JOURNEY ON

The
day ended quietly
the stars walked to their usual place
the moon came and went
sun rose sun set
I spoke to one person I did not know
an old woman soon to die
I noticed she had a kind face
                    a friendly spirit
today
was the first day of fall
soon it will be winter then spring then summer
I see with my minds eye the days unwind
If
I can maintain my balance I can carry my lamp
each day in peace
not all lives are tumultuous
some are simple and straightforward
If
I maintain my balance

EXPRESSIONS OF JOY

Raise
your hands in celebration
a life wish foretold is now born
on the road hurrying since yesterday to be at your house
welcome joy sit it down in front of you
give it water and wash its tired feet

joy comes with new legs
unclasp your hands take them from your lap
this is for you
believe it and hold it
accept it as a special gift for you
it came with the wind and we know God sends the wind
prepare yourself
tomorrow we have much to do

THE WEAK MAN

he is the down person
recognized in every land
doing the work of goliath
taking the sword in his hand to his own kind

not the bad man he thought he was
selling himself for shekels and gold
crushed against a wall his bowels emptying out

not the bad man he thought he was
taking the oath in middle age
to be good and straighten out his ways

FORGIVENESS

turn
the lamp down low
hide the hideousness of my appearance
doubt creeps all over me
only the injured knows for certain throwing knives cause accidents

I live in a new appearance
the thrower lives knowing he is the creator of grief

forty day and forty nights we both struggle against the knife

when a certain new moon came after three days of darkness
it brought Mercury to change my mind
I only ask now please send me somebody to love

COME OUT

The
darkness covers a garden of growing heads
each head with four eyes two mouths
twelve guards post one hundred and forty four doors
for a price a head will wag its tongue

Pluto comes here through a window in the floor
turning dark to light others business for the world to see

words have feet

COMMON GROUND

Children that tell grownups to be quiet
do so because the grownup acts like a child

CLOUDS

Some clouds are full of rain
they thunder and lightning
Some clouds have a deep purple cover
over a gold lining
Some clouds come late at night
step aside in the morning and let the sunshine in

Some clouds are full of imagination
make your eyes see mountains and island shores
and a garden full of vegetables with gold leaf's

THE WRONG GRIP

The
worker polished tarnished fine metals
brought them to my table as a gift
then disappeared

The
worker came late one evening to sit among invited guest
going right to left with charms and words

The
worker speaks to me privately
a stranger making promises
then quickly he is gone

   If
the worker returns it is for power
he comes as a worker of one of your guests
the worker only appears to come alone
his hand bears the mark of the wrong grip
going left to right and fewer words

POSE FINGER 2

I
HEAR CHILDREN CRYING IN THE WORLD
I
HEAR CHILDREN DYING IN THE WORLD
I close my fist with my baby fingers standing alone
I had a dream
I ran across the planet
I saw children carrying weapons of war
I saw disease and sickness
I saw viruses, the pus of poison oozing from holes
their bellies swollen from hunger
I saw boys in gangs never knowing the hand of love
I saw girls vibrating to gyrating music
interviews and advertisements slipping off their clothes
making beauty into a visionary beast
sex and nudity underneath
the mind of men switching while walking
watching women switching while walking
boys lusting with a child's mind
going up steps behind men
sex and nudity underneath
around the corner someone extra ordinary
      someone abnormal

I
saw a world of glamour and science fiction wizardry
living without spiritual fear
the eye of God is a recorder
the length of children will be measured
observe what men do to a generation sent as another gift
what sounds will come from the earth
when boys heads become men's minds
if they realize they were not taught to love
waking from dreams of murder and atrocities
men and women dead before they were born
will they commit murder and atrocities
in a world with fallen trees and howling winds
and a starving sun
what sound will come from the earth
when these children become old
will they look at their baby finger
and raise them in protest
knowing what they too have done
make a fist and raise your baby finger
for the children in this world are crying and dying
one by one   one by one

GOD'S PEACE

I
did not know when I pledged my heart and soul to
HaHiYa
that he was present until the day he stepped in my path
set pillars of good behind me and in front of me
laying a hand upon my mouth
whispered sweet words of justice in my ear

gave sight to my holy eye
set me down at his table of delights
and fed me until my heart overflowed with joy
I have known only peace since that day

SHAPES

A
man bending over backwards mending a female downstairs
an old man standing knock kneed
having the appearance of a cow out to pasture
images come to me riding by
out of the country into the city of thick lips
the debris of noise visible to the naked eye
eyes with purple circles working deep into the night
trying to figure out the meaning of a leather hexagon
beautiful bodies of females filling up at hormone pumps
taking money from men cut in half
the shape of decisions methodically influenced by Saturn
evacuating in the middle of a storm to go into the mountains
looking for peace
sitting under a tree on a side street wondering where all the time of my life went to
too many bad endings point the finger at me
I can change if I want too

SALVATION

Beware

you iniquitous, deceitful creators of devils and other lies

the day of my return has arrived.

I have picked up the bones that lay in Haran

carried them in to the valley of delights

I have returned after four hundred years in the wilderness

the circumference of my head forty degrees

I stand on a square of ninety points

in my hand I hold the sword of truth

I cut off the heads of all who oppose this witness

who march in infamy and cry foul

for they knew not the time of my arrival

delaying a journey resting in an inn where my HaHiYa

waited to slay them

I heard blood dripping on the floor

A strong woman with a knife in her hand

A son of salvation the seed of a mighty nation

Open their eyes so that there might be a witness

to speak

I stand on the lighted rock hurling words in all directions

a dervish spinning so as not to miss anyone

Be you near to the fire to get the first glimpse

Slow moving Is ra'el folds his children in a book

turning around the sun

planting and vining and pressing in to a mold

a divine spiral rising like a serpent holding a cup of oil

The sounds of trumpets fade into the night

Holy holy holy

Whose child is this whose head is so big

whose mouth utters orders

whose lips have been cast in bronze

whose heart has been sealed with gold

is this not the son of the woman with blood on her hands

who was cast aside in favor of another

Let those who see me tell others I am coming

I have come to raise bones that are not yet cold

I have come because my people have called me

No longer at a distance running towards me

we will walk the last steps together and gather more fruit than our baskets can hold

STOREHOUSE

On the horizon a red cloud sits quietly

above the cloud a river of purple stars sings

a woman feeds her child the breast closet to her heart

when you love someone very much

you give them everything you can

the red cloud reflects cuts in the skin of the sky

purple water muffles the sound of drowning

over loving can be too a heavy a rainfall even for the

largest of trees

THE RULERS

I saw two theatres of not equal size

one hand upon the others heel

coming out of a phase of darkness

changing places by degrees as the lights come up

WRAPPED

It came on a day least expected
some clouds some sunshine
a restless star in a hour of early darkness
how much work was left undone
a child I had not spoke to in a month
a child I never knew I had
the woman (the man) I love remembering our last moment of
sweetness our last moment of anger
friends searching for words trying to understand
focusing on personal fears
left alone with a thought of taking the plunge
o how sweet this dark water that claims the living
pulling them under into the deep
a day of living is a day of dying
and it comes quickly
and it never whispers I am coming for you
finish your day completely try to make it a complete wrap
close the set the movie is over

there is nothing you can hide from God HaHiYa
He is the creator and witness of all things

THE VOICE OF PEACE

I
want to die in the happiness
look in the eyes of my people
see freedom on their hearts
open the book of pleasure and remembrance
bending to no man
confessing only to serve god HaHiYa
He has sent us all and called us by name
filled us with a spirit flowing from a well of his love
I
drink from a cup of holiness
become his witness
bring peace where there has been pain
And when you hear the voice of Peace
will you not follow me
raise yourselves from the grave of deception
kiss the hand of god HaHiYa
A light before your eye

THE LEADER

Those
that are eager to lead
must take the path of servitude
seek a reluctant one
whose light and wisdom emanate
from the love of the people
Guardians rally to him quickly
receiving the word in descending order
calling the faithful to the path
the disc of holiness refined for the mind
delivered in a room of silent praise
His coming forth announced by the strangeness of the wind

SMILE

look
at yourself
see the true witness of HaHiYa's
blessing
and
smile

AND I MADE MAN

I
did not make man to break open the heads of other men
I did not make man to wound the hearts of women and children
I made man to be a witness to my joy!
From the outer most rim of myself I expressed the endless creation
I sent octave after octave of my voice spinning perpetual cycles of fire
I made suns   I made planets
I sent a cool wind to create a mist
I dug a small hole and made a sea
I made life seen and unseen
I made plants oily wet and dry
I made animals to speak and to fly
then I made man
A
simple being   I caused him to rise
A baby I made to stand
I sent octave after octave of my voice to spin man
I put him in orbit
I made him to pause and to wonder
as I unfolded myself
then I sent messengers   I sent warners   I sent geniuses
 I gave inspiration to poets
only man did I allow to create
he alone to bend and shape the octaves
I have place a man among you to set the harmony of each age, of each generation
I have set his course to turn life from black to blue
I have tuned his voice to a trumpeters call
to raise an army of holy men
I have made this creation both great and small
crickets to make night calls weeping willows bowing in grace

the camels hump the footfall of the mastodon and turtles swimming in the sea

I have made more than this for other worlds island places flying thru space paradises

men beyond human description to create worlds just like me

I created man to be a form of beauty

wisest of the wise

 a spirit companion to create with me

my creation an endless song a melody

listen mankind and sing with me

THE REGNANT

the
reign of power is held by HaHiYa
the sovereign of dignity bearing the keys to the envelope of time
on what darkest nite
on what brightest day
will the witness of glory be brought forth
arrayed in earthly finery
presented to the heavenly host
I
bow my whole head
awaiting the silence
existing in the moment of conception
watch the forces of glamour, of greed, of evil intent
the anchors that bind men to ignorance
watch them fall into the emptiness
the abyss of Not
so full is the word its pregnancy is without end
rapture fills the halls of holiness
no where in the world can this place be known
it resides in the well of the inner world of all things
the lips of plants   the smile of animals the wisps of clouds

the stars as they walk through the galaxies
all this endlessness
so far beyond the finite mind of man
one has to bow down inside himself
await the moment of silence
await the entrance of the sovereign spirit
bearing the ray of light
touching the lamp upon the top of the head
receive the candidate as alive not dead
exhaling the wind of earth
emptying the cavities of the body of fleshly things
letting go and rising into the body of the rainbow sun
HaHiYa reigns supreme
alone uninterrupted without change
without doubt
accepting only love
show yourself as one of those heavenly host singing songs of praise that never end

INTO THE HOLY CHAMBERS

The
tabernacle bends obliquely
suffering from the many years of standing
prisms of light dance on the stone floor
the alter awaits its piles of visitors
all those who seek to gain entrance
faces of children turn as quickly
as pages in the ancient text
replaced by the marching of technology
writing scribes transfigured by electronics
the minister speaks the text of today
culled from the many nights
of stargazers unfolding stories

bright stars

shaped into fallen hero's and tempest gods

not one yellowed page

marching resolutely past the north and south gates

time peels the hair off the old men

speaking from beyond the grave

old Abukan whispers ancient wisdom

in a book filled with wings

take us deep into the holy chambers

chanting for the young to rise

while the old still have breath

to witness

the replacements of men and women of power

stand up all of you

that think yourselves to be a king of your soul

BAIT

If
you have done
harm to anyone
walk don't run
let god catch you
only god can save your soul

if
a man orders you
to harm anyone
walk away from that man

Pray
that the people trapped
in a nation of pain
lift the tombstones engraved on their faces
put your feet on the road of the unshackled
and stand still
let god catch you

my dear ones
don't you know that it is god that has been chasing you
stop walking and talking
life is the line tossed into a sea we call living
we are the bait god is the hook
let him catch you
let HaHiYa celebrate
the saving of another soul
peace and peace and peace

POURING SHADE

when you discover the love of god
do not speak
he is pouring shade upon you
one word would stain the moment forever

POURING SHADE

if you had the power to pour shade
what color would you use
the color of honey because u like sweet things
or the oil of menthol because it invigorates the nose
my shade would change with the time
rose red rendering incandescent mornings
pink daffodils rising into a noon shower
an afternoon with an orange mist hanging in the air
at nite I would announce the moons etchings
semi circles surrounded by colored sunbeads
cast on the flowers of heaven
if I had the power to pour shade
I would add laughter
to see how water looks when it smiles

POURING SHADE

something forbidden has come to the world
did it begin with the tree with no leaves
pouring shade with gaps in it
 to keep the light out did they pour shade over us
not the cool shade by the banks of a river
but above the rim of the green ridge in the sun
working against slabs of quarried granite stone
have we fallen prey to massive hammers
a mile wide view of the earth's grey innards
there is no music out here
and no shade
they pour shade over us to keep us in lines
shady characters blackened by the sun
quarried like slabs of granite
there is no rest under leafless trees
where the sun burns through
to the meat of our souls

POURING SHADE

I
met
a
man
who
was
as
quiet
as
space
he said
he
got
that way
listening
to
god
pouring
      shade

POURING SHADE

god said I could touch you if you let me
and a tear fell upon my soul
lie down near that bush in the shade
and he sang in my ear with the music of crickets
come to the river and put your hand in
the water poured over me soft and cool
god then said if I pour shade over you to
strike out the rays of the sun what will you do
I said I will be still in that moment
and let you touch me

POURING SHADE

there is a fountain of blazing molten shade
when god puts his hand in the pitch
he renders it cool and moves it
sprinkling it on to creation to make colors
colors are the shade god makes to protect our eyes
colors are the shade god makes to give us beauty

HERE

I
lost my heart on a street in America
I became a spiritual traveler on the roads
here
HaHiYa put a light in my soul in America
the ocean came home
not in any other place could I have known this
this song that flows from my mind
came from home
I don't speak in another mans tongue
I don't believe as his son
the soil of America is in my bones
when I think of holy things I look next door
my ancestors are my stories of suffering
my ancestors are my stories of glory
I came to this place of passage on my own
I never had to go into the land of any ancient
people sit at their fire or climb into their bed
Their dreams are their food
I have been given grapes of my own
HaHiYa has shown me the garden
he has chosen for me
his vine is divine
it is elegant
I have been drinking for many days
I am so intoxicated I float when I walk
HaHiYa
told me to tell you only take a little sip
but I drank the whole thing
then came the words on this page
and many more so divine I found myself
a babbling bubble on the edge of time

THE ANNOUNCEMENT

Don't
be the last one
To announce
that god has forgiven you
If
there is a door that
you have to find
how will you know where to look
if there is no one left
how
will you
know the way

THE ANNOUNCEMENT

If
wisdom
had a form
I could swing on a silver thread
between
this galaxy
and the next
announcing
it
is possible
for me to
fall
forever
whether I hold on
to this string
or
not

FATHER

I
am the father
who was the son
My
day is upon me.
In my hands are the obligations
the working tools of manhood passed on to me.
Just before sunrise I meditate
HaHiYa speak wisdom to me.
When my wife looks at me let love shine
When my children call
let a smile be on their face
I
am the father
who was the son.
Now
I am a citizen
son of my people
 son of a nation
I carry iron the work men must do
I pray for the fathers that fight to keep us free
The word love beats on my chest
Across my shoulders is a harness
like my father I must learn to pull my weight
Carry the water of life
until my days are done
Embracing both sorrow and joy
arms on the same body
at night just after moonrise
I gather my family
hold them for just a little while
tell them what I know of wisdom

I
am the father
who once was the child
I
am the father
who was the son

EYES

The
eyes of creation
are closed
in deep memory
Loves breeze stirs the urge to exist
without pause
Mysterious shadows pour through
the veils of Maya
Space is the soil of creation
Elements of carbon
rise
pouring shade into boiling pits
of hydrogen, nitrogen, and oxygen
Galaxy size mountains of red yellow gas collide
splashing color on trillions of suns
Listen to the music
Listen to the music
spinning in space
The
eyes
of creation are open
in
deep memory
urged to exist
the breeze of love released
without pause
without hesitation
forever

BOOK OF TWO

Merciful

HaHiYa   I feel deeply the truth, the wisdom of that which your hand has born. I, who am only a witness see how daily that which is timeless is born anew within me. And it is as stainless as when your grace first created it. Belonging to this life are the simplicity of relationships between the light and the dark. Such is the beginning of the step of mystery. Such is the beginning of life. Such is the manifesto of relationships.

Light

gives way to darkness and is born again, forever. My feet and eyes and heart are firmly placed on this step. Its sound is the word. I am breathless, yet full. The wind is upon me serving me. It brings me the morning and the evening. It presents a multitude of worlds living and dying in the fury. The bright light of beauty and beast nurtured at the same breast. Men and women whose mouths are question marks. A tree whose branches and roots spread wildly in all directions is upon the step. Daily fruit is eaten and upon whose command? His face I have never seen. I know how its bare branches are resurrected and the fruit matured. Daily daily it feeds and serves all.

Under the revelation of grace HaHiYa   utter myself and others having gathered to consider your language. It was upon this step of light and darkness that I was taught how to go and come again. Here I was shown the come and go of life. Where the Sun of the Cry of Beauty was revealed to me and the veil of the beginning and ending of life was thrown aside. It was here HaHiYa you allowed your servant to witness the servant of all.

How

they do not know the ceaselessness of your charity, HaHiYa unmindful that should your awareness be still but for a moment they and their treasures would cease to exist. Uncaring for the hands and minds of their servants. Their rudeness exhibited even unto the trees and land and animals whose skin and innards sustain. Supposing diamonds and gold and platinum and iron as lifeless as they are.

The

same light that saw the beginning will be upon the worlds at the end. Followed by the first as last. Until each and every mouth has spoken his last until forever. It will be forever upon the consciousness of a man but only a heartbeat to the eternal, a moment of pause.

The

one that made us two came with us before we were brought to life as children, unaware, we made a way for ourselves. All was a wilderness thunder and stars. We were the eyes that saw the blood let out of bodies, even our own. The old showed us their scarred bodies and we engraved our initials on rocks and trees and they never uttered a word.

We

were the history of man and complex attitude of nature, of the sun and moon. We worked in troublesome unison all of us servants.

Giving

up daily or nightly hours for an image we lied or swore we believed in. Promising to sacrifice even our children to eagles, bears, a multitude of symbols and flags, standing long hours, children to uphold that beast which is impermanent. Bearing with our backs this slippery burden. This invention of men pretending to be a self-sustaining mountain like the heavens over our physical heads.

The

one world is an invention by men but who gives it glo? With an awful inner sway the silence of the other spoke. The one that makes us two revealed to me his symbols. It is HaHiYa that makes me glo. Each loves the other: I, the Creator, the freedom Tree, and the Creator the creation.

BOOK OF ORDER

The ears of the children are marked

their mouths so sweet and simple,

by the morning Sun

We wonder at the loud noises

the mountains fall into rivers

whose lips are painted and full

the giants have left the earth

see now what men have done.

Our children rot under the noon sun

it is our crime and we cry because they   kill us

                     because they have never known love....

Of

men and women is a pendulum whose rise and fall is manifested like a wave. They will tell you that nature is in error; that it wobbles on its hind legs like an old drunken man. Their scheme to measure the planets and in a hundred years tell you that Jupiter's motion is wrong. HaHiYa's clock is an endless song, moves without sound or waste, fulfilling each cycle completely, each step a wave spinning joyously while the Milky Way spins further out in space than they can measure. A lover's melody gracefully performed.

Of

the eyes of men and women is a clear pool whose nature all the world can see. The lover's eye bears no trilogy of thought only one clear message: my fruit is always the same. It matters not from which branch you choose. I am ripest in my season. Choose me then. My juices are then the sweetest. The wind and rains have shown me mercy and the sun, loving sun sends me showers of light, makes me right, makes me whole.

Of

the hands of men and women are roots that go into the earth. They tremble against the strain, breaking often and letting go. They work without cessation, delving deeper to feed all its members. Suffering all the pains of living. Even here we witness the mercy as we entwine the joys of touching. There is no numbness when we are building something divine.

Of

the lliving word of men and women is a tree growing from a rock unmoved by the warring noises thundering all about. Drenched by the wave of love from the lover's eye, soothed by the touch of the eternal hand. It is upon everything in Creation. A special kind of vision to the aware.

The
lliving word is a flame full of brilliant colors. HaHiYa's attributes revealed and I am a sorcerer listening to His incantations. A witness to what is truly magic, to what is so wonderfully real.

How
can we be only men, only women? The fire is infinite. It is color, vision, sound, healing: go into it. How much more is man? The lliving word awaits us with a smile. Unlike the flame that is we must become what we are.

Our
loving eye may be closed. The shadows of life to near a thing. It is said life is a high, high mountain we all must climb to become the kings and queens hidden within us. Recessed deep in our hearts with wings folded waiting for us to open up so that our souls may fly.

Over
the head of the children and the old chiefs too, over the heads of the warriors, the blind, of the emotionally drunk. Over the palaces of nations and rat holes. Over the voice of ignorance crying in the wilderness. Get in line. Get in line. The drummer calls. The drummer sings. Get in line get in line. Move he says: there is no rest. Look at the planets. They fly as if they had wings. Get in line get in line. Then the drum makes a beat. Many hear a possessive thought keeping time in their heads to what is in their pockets. Believing that death brings relief. Get in line get in line. The drummer calls again to the living and the dead: the book is being read. The choir of holy music singers let fly their voices, a crescendo on the mountain. Get in line get in line. The drummer calls in empty space: The Cry of Beauty reigns supreme. Who is the shepherd? How many days make a life? Who governs the state? Who has your heart, your soul? Where is the house of fear and how many occupy its seats? All of creation is a lliving language, the beauty of the soul. Living is an inspiration unto itself. Be alive and lose not yourself.

The
stone has no language of its own except the lines of history running through it. Life will go this way or that way, it will not be still. Untended it circles in bitterness. Too much tending and it becomes a prison without walls hyperventilating in a brown bag. We must let go to understand this is only a visit, a moment to dissolve ourselves into the body of HaHiYa..

GREASE

I
tried to carry the attention of my children in a cup that became old and worn from movement. The children were so active with all their back and forth motions. So many liquids of life pouring into its bowl it overflowed. The days and nights of emotions a dance in the mind of time. In the beginning there was simplicity. Babies with new beginnings bring the fragrances of freshness and hope and promise of what is to be the future. Life delights in its own magic, children delight in making pathways that have no fears until time begins to tear at the fabric of existence. Stumbling while walking, wiring unconnected dots to make little people copies of existing models.
Here is the story:

The children are born
take them by their feet
scorn them for their childish ways
over there in the weeds is one standing alone
different from the rest
measure his head
size him up
get him back in line
when you catch him again
scorn him for his childish ways
yesterday or the day before or the day after
he has disappeared from view
lost in the weeds
dreams in my head
are screaming my name
is the last thing he said
then he disappeared into manhood
a spirit alone....
when you catch him again measure his head and scorn him for his rebellious ways
The
wind was so hot the clouds melted into rain. The flute was warm in my mouth so I put it

down. The house was swarming with the heat of the bodies of the kids running room to room. The woman sat open legged weary from the chase, her dress falling between her legs held in the grip of a little one too short to run with the rest. The seven of us rested uneasy that whole summer. Spring rushed in the next year and the year after that. The little ones seemed to go from sprouts to shoots. The sun and wind and rain seeming to magically invest in their growth as the roots of their own interest slowly bore buds that turned into flowers full of colors I didn't understand. What kind of language is that they are speaking that seems so different from my own. What is that me and the woman have spun. The house a cocoon of flesh that stretched flesh into a human being willing to be defiant and go outside on its own, sneakily into a world of their own making, not one I had known, not one I had dreamed. In fact, outside the house the world was becoming a place I knew hardly at all.

The

cup of life I offered them to drink from was nearly full. I realized that they had drank so little, a sip here and there. From whose cup were they drinking if not mine? The woman and I would sit on the side of the bed at night and examine our hands to see if there were parts missing. We addressed our whole body for completeness and found we were whole. Those people who had come from us shared our appearance, a physical resemblance only. It was when we walked into our minds that we were awakened into reality that our children are not really our own and that we were no more than vehicles without wheels that spent such a short time with babies that had all too sudden become adults with lives of their own. I look back through time, through the years and it was revealed to me what the arc of speed is.

Dear HaHiYa

what if we had known of this opportunity in the beginning would it have made any difference at all? Who pays attention to all the words and events rising and descending. The great waves of the illusion of individual days approaching with the glory of the morning sun and the evenings of reclining moons shaping themselves into halves and quarters and slivers. The over and over of the coming of winter fore shadowing the last days of the last rites. Night has fallen on life for the old while springs toss flowers under the footsteps of the young.

Should I be shedding tears or throwing my hands in the air in exultation having suffered the experience of living.

I

have in my hands a bowl, a cup into which my life was poured. A way of knowing me that I could always look upon. It contains the liquids of the woman. It contains the liquid of the children. It contains the liquid of all that I have heard and seen and felt and smelled and known. Is this wisdom that I am witnessing? The seamless effect of love borne upon my back a treasure that others will see or is it a stake in the middle of an invisible wheel spinning me further and further away into the space that is always there between me and everyone else. The music of creation so still that the only time I ever heard it was because of a broken limb that forced me into silence in a room of solitude.

The whole affair, and it is an affair, is the symbol of love. We have made it so slippery it has taken on the image of grease and we slide helplessly in its grip uphill and downhill. The waves keep coming filled with tears and laughter trying to bring each generation into the hall of praise where the spirit of the divine presence sits in silence. Moving so swiftly it gathers up the many nations of peoples into a single body while they join together in a great voice of despair looking into the many cups pouring out their contents.

I offer this prayer to be read over the floor of destruction where the plans of undoing were constructed:

I
surrender myself
and all the contents of my cup
into the heart of HaHiYa
I turn over all the stones stored in my mind
present my elbows worn from work
show my knees and the bottom of my feet
caressed by the lips of the wind
throw open my mouth rounded by suffering
lean into tomorrow led by the light of yesterday's glory
letting go until I am no more than the same holiness that
gives light to the stars
a flower I am
bright and beautiful
fruit I am
in the hands of grace
undirected

my glance turns corners catching the sound of a whisper

a piece of smoke burning on a mountain calling my name

going up without ever asking

when I came into this world

others came also

did you send any to shake up this world?

to shape it into a knife?

to draft plans on floors of destruction?

if my voice is to be heard

if I am to be seen

prepare my cup

fill it with the water that cleans

if it is my duty to speak throw seeds onto the wind

give them a blanket on which children may sit

or a tent where many gather as one people

where the branches of divine love reach out from the tree of hope

make my body the instrument of music women dance to because

HaHiYa   has cast his net into the seas of love and caught me

I am his fish

and I lay on the beach under the sun smiling endlessly

at all who walk this way

THE DO

Creation

is a seed. The Do of creation is spin. This flesh turns.

All that HaHiYa made was made alive. The essence of all permeated by lliving space. We follow the natural Do. Created as all things to do all to the highest. To awaken the sleeping. Seeking that place within which is quiet. Daily. The Do of attracting and reflecting light. To be within the joy of peace.

Let

us make mention that the earthly life is traveling. A visitor. A soldier on a great journey to do battle with himself. Unhooking ourselves from fables to get at the truth. A brother killing his brother killing himself. A woman traveling in the midst consumed by a beguiling force speaking to her. An allegorical betrayal by men with tiny eyes sending messengers to their death. The vision of power usurped by traditions handing the reins of the chariot of truth into the hands of powerless men. Doing the bidding of horses that whisper in their ears. Performing like clowns pretending to know the way while they claim to know the day of return. How is it that HaHiYa needs a duplicate? He is plentiful unto himself without seeking permission. They fall down in ignorance whether it be day or night, January or December, 6bc or 37ad, and those that seek not ever to release from bondage and servitude former servants, trespassing against the law of the garden.

Witness

the sound of murmurings as we travel in the wilderness of freedom. Why utter against me and mine for are not these things of HaHiYa?   Has not the songs of your heart been for the remains of salvation, to know each other in peace and harmony and have you not prayed for a sip of sweet water and a road to walk upon with your mother and father sister and brother and your wife and children and best friends that is unknown by your enemy? Stand upon the Cry of Beauty if you have the strength and have been proven to immerse yourself in its word.

Soldiers

be strong. The days of asking and wanting have passed by. The Do is upon the men and women. The face of Do is in your face. The reflection of the appearance of Beauty and Wisdom and Will and Truth and Courage and Love and Recognition and Strength. The same as twins one of the spirit and one without. One above the road, one below. Come forward without fear and know the family of your family. The ancestors have posted bail in the ancient city of Zantioch, preparing for the secular of a lamb who never left footprints for man to walk through. Return over the sea to

Khamit and the sisters of her children that fly sun flags and build faces and symbols etched in stone and make peace with dream walkers that face the north and fly into the east. Withhold the army of war light has come into the world. Mark this day and hold it as evidence of the Do.

Rising

from falling as it was written in the heavens, we go into the circle as a stone. The voice of Do calls out. Rise up and place your feet next to me. Open your eyes and behold the greater things which men call mystery. I see you as you walk into the world of alone. A stone seeking bread. When all the world seems asleep darkness comes over the land.

The

hours pass without the sight of a single star. Betray not yourself soldier. Guard well this house. A family within trust their security on your vigilance. He that comes out and seeks to relieve you appears to be your brother, trust him not he is a betrayer and has been sent to maintain an order that is destined to die. Trust not his friends that come on the road for they are as he is. Obtain the horse on which they ride by pulling his mane and mount him there in the yard. Holdfast for the night is long and trying. Now the morning has come and when the family sees through the window the mount on which you have climbed many come to hold your hand.

The

mountain of love rises before you on a path filled with stones. The steed on which you ride only knows part of the way. At a high point you must dismount and leave the animal behind. So narrow and steep is the way that often you must go on your hands and knees. The darkness so great your eyes become useless. You find that only by listening to the rising winds can you make your way. A bend in the road and what appears to be a dot of light in the distance. The silence in the mountains of faith take's hold of you, a voice whispers, lets go

let's go, let's go up   within

At that moment the flood of joy flows within you.

feel this silent magic   let go   let go let go let go

peace and peace and peace

THE LIGHTED ROCK

In

the beginning was only the sound and all of creation appeared with the voice of it. I was a worshipper and like the Sun unaware of the passage of time. I was tempted and I fell both male and female. Were it not for the mercy of HaHiYa who in creation would have reached for my hand?

It

is the long journey I am on. My caring remembrance of the lovers of HaHiYa applauding and calling his name, being held in sweet esteem. Did not each pray presenting bodies before the populace as a proof? Unaware of the passage of time in which they spoke so fitted were they to the glorious work.

It

revealed those of the firm foundation. Heavenly bodies chanting, swing in the firmament. The garden of the tribe of Nad. A ram trailing two little ones and she goat with twelve horns drinking from the well. I hear the sounds of man running to and fro. Then my eyes beheld the well and nearby a rock. We knelt in prayer. Then came fire out of the rock to burn the souls of strong men. The same rock that was given to the messengers from the hand of HaHiYa. There was a silver gate leading to the rock and all around it was formed in the wilderness. Forty steps to the mount thereof with ninety eyes. I beheld a mother holding her leg. A scorpion had left its mark.

Approaching

from my place of hiding I administered healing drawing the poison into myself. Then a voice called to us from the formless. We went into the mist discovering there a step made of pure gold in the form of a circle. There I saw a book whose name I cannot repeat. We slept on this step ten days. Then the voice awakened me and the mist was no more, the same of the circle and the mother. I prayed then greatly for my fear was great. Suddenly my body shook as the ground beneath me lost its footing. A large valley opened up. This valley had the shape of a triangle. I was shown a book filled with symbols one on top of another and the meaning also. Again, I went to sleep. Someone said I slept one hundred and twenty four days and nights.

Now

the Creation was truly different. The gate was behind me and the rock before me and millions all about of animate and inanimate, the seen and the unseen. Here also was water. I stood on a path touching my hands left and right north and south to the body that was before me. My people surely HaHiYa has filled the way with greatness. Upon the rock was the sweetest name. Binding me and the creation to its firm hand. Even though the planets fly in space the birds wing into the atmosphere. So too are we taken up. Our words carrying us to the Creator. The Rock, which was without form and dark, was now whole and full of light. The light of it a Fire and it consumed me, filled me. My faith is on this Rock. My spirit is on this Rock. My children were found upon this Rock that they might flourish. All who are with me this day have come pass the gate and dwelled with me on this Rock. It is above the firmament and everlasting. HaHiYa's mercy, through His grace I have witnessed the image of the face that supports my step, filled with rhythms of the circle and symbols of the word. No man has witnessed the lighted Rock or made his way past the gate. I AM as sweet now as a lover's rose. It is HaHiYa who has shown me this favor. His hand made what was upside down face side forward, the harmony of sublime revelation. HaHiYa has given me a rock whereby I may stand. A Rock that is not physical but the word coming from the wilderness. The same symbol Moses rose with to still the small voices at his hips, sounds of dying men and women despising me for my words. Going hard by the river or near to the city limits the presence of the lighted Rock seems to fly East and West in my hand singing praises HaHiYa I will praise your name in the eternity whatever worlds you send me

I am truly your sacred lover

CREATION

is energy. Its fuel is will that compels it onward. Creation is in orbit of itself. The orbit is love holding itself together coming not apart.

I

am set sail for the positive oceans and worlds. I have only my thoughts on the ship I sail. I have purposely discarded everything of yesterday. It is a new day and a new sun dawning. This is the greater light for me to grow under. The only reflections I see are the ship and the sky. I have the sun and moon and stars. Behind me are the city and thoughts of yesterday. Soon they are out of sight.

On

these uncharted waters no man can travel with his companions as new waves greet each moment. Each wave a sign to learn from. Intuition and will are your guides. The waters go everywhere. There are a multitude of islands which provide rest for short periods then the waves come again drawing you on. Whispers fill the air tugging the heart closer to the island of your desire. Refreshing the mind with its fragrance. I have been to these islands in the firmament. The truth is that these islands exist in all the worlds; each lovelier than the one before.

The

aspect of creations newness, the unexpectant always around the bend, just out of sight. How could any man take the thoughts of the old world to the new world. We must follow the next step higher and higher, deeper and deeper. Hold a steady course, forget about the cities with false glamour. They are not endless nor are their makers. Think not that life is easy. It is so liquid it spills. More liquid than the obvious prison that holds the criminal. More liquid than the hurt of lost love. The dawn brings us many lovers with which we entertain ourselves when on that sea. We are liquid when we sail by ourselves. Hard to get a hold on. Hard to keep still the thoughts that flow from us in us.

Creation

is a lliving language. Its image awakened us to life. Alone our thoughts go freely. Feed yourself by the bay of HaHiYa. The old way is a ball and chain. Listen. It is merely a rattle. No longer the smell of freshness to keep the patient's attention only the feeling of the end. All affairs are worthwhile. All affairs come to an end. Leave the land willingly, take to the waters.

Follow the uncharted to know ourselves.

Men

remind each other of the old themes, of the old stories. Life provides us with storms to lose its appearance. It is a puzzle we pit ourselves against.

On

each resting place are lessons. Shake away the dust to let light in. Gather the words of the flowers that are in front of you. A rare beauty lives a moment or so it seems. Reach out your hand when the stream passes by, receive what is yours.

By

Himself did HaHiYa create the creation. By himself did HaHiYa endow the prophets with sweetness. The Suns light given to the moon. Sailing in the ocean of them catching adventurous children impregnating them with the fire of a hot wind.

HaHiYa alone is the essence
HaHiYa alone is the fuel…

BOOK OF THE GREYHEADS

Into

the eyes of the nation HaHiYa has spread the vision of His boundless love. The season of change ripples on the shore of the words torn from the throats of mankind. HaHiYa forgive us our weakness. Forgive them the lies they grow in our ears. Security has run away from us.

Now

the ignorant cry out feeling the abandonment of the nation. The loneliness of the world without the Father's great spirit to wade in. Who can be the Creator? Far flung are the worlds. Distant are the workers from the truth of this earth. What of the wind that has assembled among the heads of our children?

Here

strides the great nations of the earth. Transforming the gift of light into destruction. The nations have become doddering old men, absent mindedly seated at a table giving out orders to servants that despise them. Servants that listen to their raucous laughter, observe their indecent behavior. Servants that smile and assist them in degenerate actions. They are blinded by their own grandeur their armies and weapons useless. HaHiYa has sealed the covenant with His new people. While the nations meet in council, scientist talk about the latest experiments, the hour of HaHiYa passes them by.

HaHiYa's

vision has spread into the nations and they stare as if dead. The leaders have poisoned themselves. A rulership of thought of nineteen centuries. The Book of Plenty laid before them to end want and desperation. The West rises each day as a soulless giant. The work of mad men.

Today

millions share the vision of the video. Loving themselves they market this image over the earth. Subjugating the people into this nocturnal dream.

Behold

the day of days has dawned to cast aside the desire for darkness, to give men a reason to believe that salvation is truly of the spirit. Come to the Cry of Beauty. Awaken the children living in the world of abandonment.

The impact of war, of economic misery mirrors the agony of the government's shadow, marshaling them into action. They request order lost to them because they lack the proper tool. They threw away the tool and it is lost to them. The people will only be blinded so long. The bark of bickering, of falsehood, and treachery a reward for pain and suffering.

Without the proper tool none can speak. A horn appears falsely proclaiming salvation. Deceiving the people with honors and awards. The nations say: we are the gods of this world. In our hands resides the Book and its words carry the works for heaven on earth. We are making the future today. Come let us build the new world together. Let the glory of our science show forth and we will dispose of war and envy and treachery and human suffering. This and much more will be said to redeem them from destruction but not one word will be said of the purpose, of the proper tool. How foolish for men to devise a plan to resurrect the physical, to remake cities, adorn them, make them shiny and fill them with the stench of dead bodies.

Wise men of science and government you are not the salvation, not ever.

The children see the video, feel the fear and the loneliness. They witness the desperation and the treachery. They learn through neglect the world is amiss. Their heads rehearsing the lessons of the nations. The video with its head up, a beast saying the same thing for twenty four hours, seven days a week, rehearsing them over and over. Many marvel at the light in the children's' eyes. Even more are they not amused by the words of their mouths. The specialness of this generation a candle on the road.

Let us proclaim salvation, the greyheaded children, their hands extended, reaching for a ray of gold light, the spirit of HaHiYa. The light created by a special child to arouse the shaken. Light in the form of an eagle, in the sign of, placing the spirit of the witnesses on the wings of divine love. The stage is set to remove the wicked from his post. Count them the unbelievers, know them by name.

The children of   HaHiYa   the special ones touch the spirit to make man a loving family. Witnesses to heal the world fulfilling the covenant. Glory spilling on the ground, the roots of trees drinking greedily, swollen fat from the light within them. Bless this time, it is precious, complete of itself.

I
make witness that the Cry of Beauty lives and reveals wisdom to whom wills it....

peace and peace and peace

THE UNION

>   the female: flowers, wind, and water
>   the male: land, trees, and fire
>   bound together to inspire, to create...

The
Spirit sings upon each Word. And it is like fire,
the searing touch of love that goes unbending. Oh
the warmth of joy radiates at the point of the source.
HaHiYa   here or there?
Not of the fire, in it? The ever present mystery. Within
and without the steps of wisdom, the herbs of the fields,
the land, names of brilliant fire, stones. Each step an
endless journey.
Sing
to us now concerning the land and the flowers, the female and the male. From a single point man was inspired into being, the atom of form, multiplied and filled with the cup of devotion until the time when deception entered.
Together
the male and female labored, drawing food from the earth. And these were the generations of physical strength. The hunters and tillers of the soil and this was the first science, when men wandered further from the Spirit of the Word. It was naming form after themselves and this was the first science. The generations of the ground, the time of males.
These
were the generations of conquering, of exploring, of Brotherhood. And the land and the male was dominate. Science began to subdue the earth. Men worked to fulfill the promise of peace on earth. Complicating and confusing what was simple and divine with rules and deception posturing glamour and possessing, reducing all that has a name to its monetary value; a raging torrent of imaging, held together by the magic of human faith, a breathless invention puffing its way into oblivion. The science of men taking on the garb of science fiction, denying the Spirit, dividing the road until the earth and men have become strangers. And what of the female during these many generations. Shunted aside into lesser roles of obedience. A partner with well-honed tools, a

watcher, assuming an unaccustomed role at the table with men. A changing of the sentries, a change in positions. The female in a role of freedom, to flower at last in the sunshine of this day. The flow of her waters adding a touch of art, slowing down the pace, observing the handiwork of men from a female eye.

It

is a new season in Creation, a movement of union, of coming together. Assembling the pieces, calling forth the workers, the soljahs, to step past resistance using the tool

jointly, to sit at the table as one, to decide under the light of the inspiring Spirit.

I

give you these words to proceed by:

WE are joined by the love of HaHiYa

charged by the fire of His eternal love

I come upon you the flower, you come upon me the land

hand to hand

the rhythm of our footsteps unfettered

possessing nothing not even ourselves

sharing our hopes and our dreams

we accept one another to share the light of good days

we accept this walk together to carry each other

to nurture us through the times of light and darkness

wrapped in the body of love we present to each other

these gifts:

patience labor celebration

until we are consumed by the earth

giving our commitment to these sacred vows.

May God HaHiYa Bless Us

increase our abundance

make our generations fruitful

multiplying us,

receiving our spirits overflowing with joy on the Great Day of the end of life

Peace and Peace and Peace

THE WINDS OF CHANGE

A
man, his family and members of his tribe forcibly removed from their homeland are stripped of the past. Groomed and fired by time they approach the modern world without spiritual tools. This modern world empty as men seek to fulfill their needs with physical foods. Send out the raised ones of the heavenly abode into the towns of men and call forth the begotten of HaHiYa. Seek out the disease of corrupted hearts, disrupt it, call my people to stand up and be counted. The day of days is upon the earth.

They
have come upon you, the poor and the hopeless. One hand behind their back holding the promise of heaven upon the moment of death; the other hand searching the depths of your pockets. Asking you for emotions and dressed affairs from those that can least afford it.

It
is no wonder the children reject it, it is empty. A voice in the nite calling and calling. Promising to reveal a body in the morning light. Unable to stop the fighting among us like men atop a mountain of confusion.

HaHiYa
is for the people. HaHiYa (the hand of life), the point of peace, of inspiration. HaHiYa's existence free of temples and statues. His message carried upon the wings of the Cry of Beauty, the light of His Word, the ever-expanding lliving language. Present eternally, ceaseless in raising and inspiring his guides, the Koba. Each with the proper tools to refresh a fallen humanity. Pursue the moment of light, hasten to the footstool of this guide and receive the moisture of divine love.

The
Word of this is food. It is a table heavily laden with sweet meats and wine. Each gesture a dip in the eternal.

The
speech of HaHiYa for the poor in spirit, prisoners of self neglect. Search not your pockets for a rental payment. Bow not before any man. Bow not before any symbol that men say is a representative of HaHiYa. The creation and all its parts are the symbol. Trace the history of all that you see and hear and the trail leads to the same self emanating power, the light of HaHiYa The Hand of Life.

Divide

not the people, not your family with false words or anger, repeat The Point of Peace morning and nite, invite the power of love on the Half Moon; save fifteen cents of each bill you earn; consume only water on Monday; join you all house to house as a family to share your wisdom and your tools for prayer and for planning; celebrate the third moon, each and every one as a tribe under the light of HaHiYa, for reunion and meditation, interpretation, for government; keep your history; the third moon celebration for four days and upon the last day after government enjoy the fruits of labor in song and dance; to keep the spirit fresh and alive. Let the artist and scientist share their discoveries with all and then separate in peace until you meet again in three months. Share your commerce among one another and others so that in all ways you might enjoy the company of one another and seek the Way without earthly encumbrance

OCMABA: BOOK OF PRAYER

All
those who sit at the table of HaHiYa
know my name
They are among those sitting in the boat
that left its mark in the Milky Way and
all the gates of Heaven and all its divisions
They know the steps on which my name was traced
I gave unto each tribe my symbols in his own word
in his own time
Raised my servants and separated my children
into divisions to serve me
Unto this day when I make my word known to you
Call me by name
As I raised a tree in the heavens so shall I raise a man
to speak
This man is my flower my tree my root and my branch
He is my full moon in the galaxy of my mind
More than you can know
Would you inquire more?
I have given to my servant all that you can know
Would you inquire more?
Know you the meaning of bones under the field
and frozen hearts on the tundra?
When man comes to know a part of my creation my foot steps have already been covered
by the dust of time
If man knew my beginning then he would know all
I
have sent this one among you to say my words
Do with this one what you have done in the past?
What have you to do with my name and my comings and goings
Your deceit in creation has not gone without notice

both before and after

HaHiYa is the hand of life

Seso is my Prophet

Who will stand against my servant? the unbelievers

ama

KOBA

HiYa

I am the witness you have summoned

I am he that saw the Cry of Beauty

I saw your fingers in the heavens swinging the suns and moons and planets without end

I heard your sound the wind in clouds and on the ground

I saw your coat of many colors the flesh of moving and growing things

I bow before you in my mind where you have come to take me to meet my spirit

this path is dark and full of mystery in front of me

all that is behind me is arrayed in light

I am a carver with a scalpel shaping myself into a dream HaHiYa alone has the picture of

I

bend myself to your will HaHiYa

I pray day and night now that you have summoned me

I hold out my chest to be struck upon by those with blind hands

I raise my voice in the cottage of the poor

whose hinges on the door squeak

whose roof leaks

whose children's eyes sink

the sounds of war rage on the street

Not more than seventy souls raise themselves to the one true light

they come before me each with the voice of the Cry of Beauty on their lips

I

pray that we will not be discovered before time reveals

us as babes still in the womb of HaHiYa

ama

2.

Four hundred years passed like forty years

Forty days and forty nights

The scared sent ones to await us at a place to replace us

A sign of a tribe with stone heads

poisoned by arrows fashioned by hellish men

Look at the enemy of my people

They have been put in charge of us

this was a time of our puberty

Have they acted wisely?

What has been done to our genius'?

What is the heart of the man that spilled his seed in the belly of our women?

What did the enemy of my ancestors say to our prophets

they asked the government and the church to join hands

Who speaks to release us from an ugly bondage?

I

pray that HaHiYa forgives us all

I pray that the thickness of our necks is cooled by holy water falling like manna from heaven

What will my enemies say when HaHiYa invites them in to talk?

When they say that men decided which men have souls and which men don't?

Will we see the fathers of ten generations who were

masters serving our ancestors from a table laden with grapes

surrendering themselves to the will of HaHiYa

HaHiYa

I pray that when you come after us we will be ready

waiting in the fields ready to go at that moment or

suffer death because of a double mind

ama

3.

HaHiYa

I offer thanks at your table

accept this harvest from the field

my plate is filled

May this food acknowledge your blessing

to strengthen me to work in your name

ama

4.

I

awaken each day knowing that it will come

with a sun and a deep blue sky

or dark clouds with rains

Each day that comes is a treasure of creation

Affixing every planet to move in accordance with its

sun to receive a measure of light

One night my eye was opened

I saw a faraway place with a rainbow colored sun and a planet with a lavender sky

with yellow and black trees and pink dirt and beings that were beyond my description

I fell among them at the foot of a child

we spoke: what are you?

HaHiYa spoke: did you think I made you alone

ama

5.

You

sent me into this world

an old man told me what he thought of me

For many years I lived thinking
you never thought of me at all
I
lived in fear of other men
fearful of what they knew that I seemed not to know
their steps so much longer than mine
I
saw shadows of their luxuries as they passed me by
but no one told me about all they had lost to make these gains
The old man lived a simple life
loved by all the children of his family
none of them had ever gone astray
Sweet   Sweet   HaHiYa
I have come to know that this spot which you have
given me is one of rare beauty
I am not a king or a prince
I am not a man of recognition that runs a state
or a corporation
but I did submit my heart to the Captain of a ship that sails in eternal waters
I pledge my allegiance to HaHiYa
honoring the ring of faith
with which He has crowned me
Love is a shadow of other men bending their knees
to HaHiYa
I walk in bright sunlight
knowing my steps are not measured by what I possess
I have made my daily deposit
Water in a well
drawn by a rope tied to the waist of the most high
I joined the order of Ocmaba
and became a free man and Koba (teacher)
Behold
you iniquitous, deceitful creators of devils and other lies

the day of my return has arrived.
I have picked up the bones that lay in Hapi
carried them into the valley of delights
I have returned after forty years in the wilderness
the circumference of my head ninety degrees
I stand on a square of ninety points
in my hand I hold the sword of truth
I cut off the heads of all who oppose his witness
who march in infamy and cry foul
for they knew not the time of my arrival
delaying a journey resting where a woman
waited to slap them
I heard blood dripping on the floor
A strong woman with a knife in her hand
A son of salvation the seed of a mighty nation
Open their eyes so that there might be a witness
to speak
I stand on the lighted rock hurling words in all directions
a dervish spinning so as not to miss anyone
Be you near to the fire to get the first glimpse
Slow moving Saturn folds his children in a book
turning around the sun
planting and vining and pressing in to a mold
a divine spiral rising like a serpent holding a cup of oil
The sounds of trumpets fade into the night
Whose child is this whose head is so big
whose mouth utters orders
whose lips have been cast in bronze
whose heart has been sealed with gold
is this not the son of the woman with blood on her hands?
who was cast aside in favor of another
Let those who see me tell others I am coming
I have come to raise bones that are not yet cold

I have come because my people have called me
No longer at a distance running towards me
we will walk the last steps together and gather more fruit than our baskets can hold
 ama

THE POINT OF PEACE

I
take this oath locking it in my heart
awaiting sunrise to receive the light of
        HaHiYa
illuminating my consciousness
filling my body with light
the winds of change are upon me
I descend into myself
I stand upon the lighted rock   I kneel here and pray
I rise and sing witnessing the Cry of Beauty
I close my eyes and feel the silence of the morning
the point of peace.
I will carry this silence with me through the day
share it as a greeting
I will bring it to my night prayer and repeat it
the Oath   to receive the light of
        HaHiYa
morning and night
I will know the silence

the point of peace....
ama

THE CYCLES: ARMAGEDDON

Within

the context of each generation are those things which come springing forth of the will of humans. It is the Legating of one experience after another. The good word comes walking gently to its place. Forming itself into a circle of blessing. At a distance a crowd of clown's spawn's laughter holding banners and making displays that the light has not come and the hours of leisure are many, even more than days but years in which there is enough time for play. Their smile a deception upon themselves and all who know when the clock is ticking away the next moments announcements. The space between the seconds an award of the silence to reflect on individual existence.

Here

comes a moment of the generation begat betwixt a fall into uncertainty and a second look over the shoulder of a man who is wondering about his direction. Stepping from the house of life into the business of activity and the dance of daily events is a series of pictures of behavior. Herding the young onto the paths of migration so that they will learn the ways forged by the old. Giving them signs and symbols of the times, past and present. Occasionally witnessing the camps of the lost looking at a pathway whose tracks wander from the main road. Others that have stopped moving as the herd passes them by their eyes not seeing anything in particular. Searching within themselves who they are, what might they become. One foot on the main path the other on land of the wandering seekers.

On

a building the sounds of hammers and machinery whirl in the air. Driving thuds erect frames covering them with skins that reflect modern life. Birds launch themselves from manmade perches looking for crumbs tossed by passersby. The elegant life adorning a great nation Legating a thread of arrogance. This thread made of strands of supposed loftiness. Colors blending to make one whole appearance.

The

blue color of indifference, the green color of unshared wealth, the red color of power, the yellow color of lonely hearts, and the brown colors of separation. Symbols of their disease. A rainbow thread born in nations overflowing with the sounds of all that they have gathered from the earth. Men spending time in the counting houses adding up tomorrows bounty on dark days while the clouds roll in filled with thunder and lightning. They are consumed with the sounds of the hammers they have hired and counting, their ears locked on what occurs in their heads and the heads of their associates.

The

globe is covered with a moving shadow. It is Legating a generation of tears. What need has any man in the midst of suffering for a prophet to come and tell him what he already knows. Will the prophet say I have come to save you from your suffering? The hungry mother will say I know this already. Even the child of suffering expresses the wisdom of knowing. Go to the rich man, go to those whose harbors are receiving the wealth of nations. Go to their large houses and to their cities. Then walk among the poor, the different ones and see what their blessings might be. The poor laborer here is the poor laborer among other people in other nations. May the common prayer be offered on earth among men. The container of suffering is cast in the same mold. Its mouth turns by degrees to be understood by the many nations that offer service. Each nation in its turn coming with corn, beans, amethyst, diamonds, gold, cobalt, oil, incense, berries, nuts, rice, coffee, nitrates, the soil of the earth and its trees. Coming to the great nations that have divided the globe into regions for themselves. Spoiling their daughters and sons with parades of many things bought for them because of so many laborers.

Where

did the good spirit go while men did these things? The human will is a separate thing. It was Legat in the soul with the appearance of man. Goodness formed itself into a circle of light beyond the shadow of things moving to and fro. Stepping off the pathway of traditions of the herd. Migration after migration came to the waters on the well trodden path. These waters filled with the debris of human experience. The herd trudges through them going to the next watering hole. On a cycle so predictable the blind lead them. No need to open their eyes, the bite of their teeth vicious warning to any who stray. Talking against and ignoring or driving from the main body those who question or rebel and desire a new direction. The oldest guard holding the line against the young coming closer to the front to make change. A terrible moment Legat by terrible people or so the story goes.

The

speed of the moving shadow increases as it nears birth. Its color a lazy purple with flashes of lightening filled with men of an unusual nature. Preparing to launch themselves with the fury of aliens not of this world. Angered by what they see has happened to their world. This child Legat in a tempest. The head of his mother bald from worry, the body of his father crying in a shallow grave. The voice of his ancestor's ring in his ear. Smoke comes out of his mouth because smoke is on the hills and valleys. For this one life is a furnace. He prepares his camp in the wilderness where there are no roads. The shadow, the unknown squirming to locate a place where they might fit.

The
face of the West is overcast by the suns orange light. The promise of fruit imminent in the womb of hope and things that are to be. Wind churns through the nite, nails that have anchored the soul of a new beginning are released. Making its way from the mountain the footsteps of a new nation Legat itself. Armed by poetic justice the fourth element rising slowly on the world stage. Brown eyes and kinky hair, masculine lips and strong backs, sinewy hands and a consciousness crackling with the endurance of suffering and a heart shaped by a mother's patience and a father's wit. A witness to a new kind of man. His mission messianic. His color a radiant golden-brown hue, reposed in the word of the west.

Mothers prepare their daughters to be wives.

Fathers prepare their sons to do battle.

The
lower plain holds a vast army of men whose vested armor has seen the ravages of seventeen centuries. A rolling field of dust spins an army whose vested armor has seen the ravages of more than thirteen centuries. On the middle plain encamped on all sides the thorn of Egypt thrusts it's self repeatedly. It's borrowed vested armor has seen the ravages of more than forty centuries. A single drum beat and the call of a horn signal the rise of the next participant. His vesture a little cloth having seen the wisdom of more than eighty centuries. Coming into his place by request. A request from life itself. When men are needed then they are born to seek and fulfill the task.

To
answer the questions, to make solutions the chemical dynamic of Creation responds with human elements. Time has come knocking with its four bells, each bell a different color, each bell set to its own time. Ringing until the final note sounds marking the end of its time. Marked on the path drops of blood display impatience and selfishness. The smells of anger, jealousy, and greed sift in the air. The ideas of a more ancient way collide headlong into a rising column of technological freedom. Within each of the first three camps rancorous words struggle against one another each trying to convey a human concept of right and wrong amidst the backdrop of expanding scientific knowledge amidst theological limitations and practice. Sparks flare from the heat of disagreement as more heads enter the fray butting one another. Armed with impatience and righteous indignation the circle of the dance of death rattles its sabers. The open display of military might and scary tactics lights up the sky. A time of doom is declared as the points of difference reach a plateau of human abuse. No one wants to feel left out or left behind. Many of the leaders withdraw their bitten and painful fingers.

Lodged

in the fourth camp are the elements of a new way. The journey across a human plan of barriers. Fixed forever with the mark of their appearance. Brown eyes and kinky hair. Presented to many as soulless without a god of their own. An outcast in the world for four hundred years. Witness the tribe of improvement move to positions of vision. The sound of Armageddon thunders in the distance as many prepare for a battle of epic proportions. Yet, the roadway is being cleared as the approach of the lliving word hits the trail. Nature leans back in reverence accepting the will of truth. A great moment of joy clings to the breath of all things. A beginner, an original form walks forward. The clanging of armor of the four camps undergoes a change as the fray deepens daily. The noise of their campaign interrupted by a Captain of each house. The ears of legions receiving messages from home of an original form walking forward. His vesture the word of his mouth, a flame of endowment thousands of years old. Speaking in a new way. When the world pauses the sound of his voice is clearly heard. Many that claim to know were dumbfounded. They did not know the words contained in his book, THE CRY OF BEAUTY, and he spoke continuously for many days:

Those

that would separate men one from another have a vision of their own. Those that seek to make women subjects of men have a vision of their own. Those that seek to make children adults without the passage of time have a vision of their own. Those nations that take only have a vision of their own. One tribe that sets a barrier against another has a vision of their own. One man that feeds another who is able to feed himself has a vision of his own. The temple of the human body is the most sacred temple on earth, it is not to be defiled or treated in an irreverent manner. It is holier than any other place because it is there that the spirit resides and raises man from animal to peace. Free will is a state of spiritual consciousness and benevolence, and the citizen who exercises it plants it like a seed and tends it like a sacred garden. For each step widens the waves that flow from it. Seek wisdom that the seeds journeys find as little entanglement as possible. Love ripens all conditions and will in time rub the heart until it as fine as a field of soft sand, each grain the lessons of participating in the experience we call lliving. HaHiYa is the name of god. IIe is the bearer of the field we call Armageddon. HaHiYa is the bearer of all that is to come in the new field. Armageddon is a field of fruition. On its corners lie the borders of rebellion both old and new. The field of peace and the field of obligation and truth.

The

Camp of ancient tribes that separated themselves from one another and the camp of suffering

set aside as descendants of MISERY and other nonpeople selected only for their use in fields where they would not get in the way. The field of armageddon little more than a dark cloud of unfinished human business. ARMAGEDDON, a word meant to impress, a tiny river on a dot on the map of creation. It is the fourth bell and is the shortest. The dragon of its fire already smoldering in the ocean of its own ruins. The field of fruition, of armageddon, is a replanting. The expansion of man takes notes of a cleansing and removal of barriers of the four corners. A language in the minds of all people that makes everything current. The nature of this garden newly laid stretching far into the heavens above. Welcoming man to be a spiritual soldier and creator in his new garden. Once again given the directive: replenish the earth and beyond and multiply.
Man
has set himself upon a stage reflecting the crossroads of many generations, of many deceptions, and a crucible of blood given by those who chose joy over misery, sacrifice over greed, human kindness over treachery, and the spirit of god HaHiYa to be good, to multiply and replenish the earth not to plunder or for individuals to coerce men and women or use tactics of intimidation to conquer territories and establish regimes of crime and puppet states. The wealth of the earth is incomprehensible and is virtually inexhaustible if the garden inherited by each generation is properly tended. Man has no garden that he has created or soil or water or air or sun, not even the hands he uses to feed himself or build his houses did he imagine. Nothing that exist in creation did man imagine but HaHiYa has allowed man through free will to use his imagination, to become inspired, to use logic and observation, to become aware of creations possibilities and fulfill his desires even if they have not always been right. Armageddon is the right time for man to come to an understanding that man is not just man. Not races or cultures of separate genius but a family that needs diversity to speak about all that man comes to know as new and different. If we miss this chance then we go into the long night of darkness, the road where there is less hope and more misery. Man's destiny is not of this earth but deep in the holiness of his soul
peace and peace and peace

FIRST MESSAGE

When

the words began to formulate they came murmuring. Unsure of themselves not knowing where to begin. A seed blowing in the wind with a voice unrecognizable. Carried over the waters of time settling in a village, in the mind of a child. Generation by generation growing among the wild things it was always known to be beautiful. Then it spoke in a clear voice to one who could hear its message. Gather those that believe and make of them trees to stand alone under the canopy of bright stars. Rain falls from the heavens on the center of their heads soon they too will come to know the First Message.

The First Message

came to me murmuring. Questions without answers. How do I know to believe? What should I believe? How do I proof what I believe? How old is believing?

I

look to my underself. The lliving part of me that was me before I came to this world and that part of me that goes on after I leave this world. My soul cries out that I am more than just a man. How do I know to believe? If this creation ceases not to be and the natural things here play out the seasons going on forever, coming and going, playing as if dead only sleeping through the winter months, coming to life with the spring thaw.

It is a great joy to see the rising of babies whether they be flowers or animals or the warmth of the wind, the turning of the arcs of planets lowers and raises the lights influencing the flow of life. Changing the frozen water to rivers overflowing their banks to feed the thirsty. Nourishment abounds and the stirrings of hope for the brightness of the next day await their entrance. For those that live in the world of instinct there are no questions if a ray of life comes in spring and that the next round of beginning is only a year away as man marks time. The bones of all those who have come and gone litter the fields and it is a truth that requires no speech. What was left on the road can be read as each step mounted one upon another the fruits of genius, machinery inspired by a divine imagination.

I

look upon the past and see men and women diving into pools of unknown depth seeking treasures. Some of them never rose again but others came to the surface on islands of a new world.

How

long had these islands existed before they were added to the list of things not known before?

A woman carrying oil to make fire, a man with a machine with a motor flying through the air fueled by liquid oxygen.

The
air of believing surreal. Making the impossible possible. Leaping ahead to islands that some said could not exist. Rain that falls on the head opening valleys filled with rivers filled with symbols and dreams, faraway places soon to be near but not as men mark time. The spring season of creation when all comes anew flying gently as a butterfly. Magnificent in its array of colors, fresh from a cocoon of mutation. Going into a state of mummification, self-wrapped and unwrapped by natures time clock.

I
believe the First Message. It comes upon the stairway talking in a low voice and when I have seen it face to face I know. The First Message is to know. The magic of all this lliving is to know. Men believed they could do things, using the vehicle of the imagination to soar into millions of fantasies and dreams. Merging science and religion into legions of speculation, piled high with hope and disappointment, experimentation, and prayer. Yet, all was at an end until the hands reached out into the unknown, diving from the cliffs into the pools of mystery coming ashore on the island of what was only thought to be a dream or some imagination. Stand here and see.

Watch
the
spirit of HaHiYa
unfold the new extension of creation
It is wide and it is deep and it flows as a river should into a valley of knowing
and an island filled with relief.
Peace and Peace and Peace

TRAVELING TO THE WORD

How
far will you travel to reach the Word. There should be no hesitation when your name is called. God loves what he has created why should you allow fear to play on your heart, enter your dreams or cloud your mind with the doubts and thoughts of other men and women. Within his gate there is no harm or foul plays or schemes.

There
is a table set by many men whose plates are fattened by the storehouse of darkness. Those whose code is danger seek it out no matter the distance. Wise cracking smiles crease their lips. The red lights of lust sparkle in their eyes. They have the best of dress from the houses of labels. The smooth sound of gold flows around their wrists and necks. Fingers and toes and ears flash with diamonds and pearls and rubies and emeralds and other fine stones. They fly anywhere in the world without hesitation completing or assigning men and women to fulfill a deadly mission. Trafficking in intrigue they are the mighty ones on earth. Their hearts and minds on a spiritual vacation that never seems to end as their power over the earth's treasures ascends daily up manmade steps of royalty and principalities.

How
far will you travel to meet the word? It is here you know. It is calling your name. Speaking to the lone men and women traveling in the shadows of the men of power. Not able to fit the design of men something else on their mind. They see the fashions of men as withering flowers whose roots are weary fevered by the search for water of a more heavenly nature. Even the criminal cannot do wrong twenty four seven. Even the criminal seeks peace and happiness. His soul darkened because he is his own wrong path.

When
the news comes it arrives with the suddenness of the morning sun. Bringing the water of life, carrying it to the mountain top. Waiting there for those that find themselves in the desert of men's desires. Turning away from the deceit, turning toward the mountain of light.

The
hour of promise is but an hour or so it seems. The presence of its rays burning a hole in the less fortunate, the unprepared and men caught in the act of living off the storehouse of darkness. Unable to get out in time to witness the other life. There hour endures for many days.
Even the proud and the mighty fall into the wayside.

The
day of travel is the obligation. To go quickly, traveling by nite, traveling by day. Entering the land of the great mystery of tribulation and adoration. The wind carries a fragrance of holy fruit. The road itself sings as the traveler ascends step by step. The face of nature's four seasons pass in a single day. The spiritual famine recedes bit by bit.

Crossing
this wilderness onto a plateau where a garment of deep colors awaits you the candidate of light. Here the wind is silent. A heavenly hush falls over you when you see the old footprint. Your eye sees the old footprint leading away into the upper mountains. A thought of all that has gone before descends upon you the traveler, the candidate. There is no need to take a final look back at the life you have completed. For the traveler it has passed away in one glorious moment. There is a name on the old footprint. The impression of its mark a reflection of your own footsteps.

How
far will you travel to reach the word? Follow the old footprints and know what it really means not to be a pillar of salt.

TRAFFIC

What

men do begins as a child in a family and the family of men rising upon the bones of ancestors. The speaking bones of ancestors. The speaking bones of ancestors have two mouths: one that speaks loudly of things that are known; the other a whispering mouth speaks of things hidden or recently discovered along the way.

The

family moves in circles one round the other speaking loudly of the things known. The ancestor bone sticking out of the mouth of the mother and father, the grandmother and grandfather, the aunts and the uncles. Each of them speaking loudly about what was spoken before. Preparing the road the child is to walk upon.

The

child displays the gifts of speech it has been given. What is yes and what is no. If the child has come with the gifts of the arts the voices will flow. Some will come with an understanding of the ground and all the things it contains. Some will see the workings of the sky and beyond. A great number will have the habits of ants and bees while others will assume the positions of giraffes and the more special ones will fly like eagles.

Yet,

it is the traffic of men and women that contain traditions that require periodic adjustments. After many generations the light of the crystal stares as if dead. Be prepared then for the special children that will come past your door and see the work of HaHiYa upon the field in which the earth is entering.

All

that was in the wagon of traditions, including the drivers, the old man and the old woman, the relics and books of the things that they held dear, stuck in the path that became muddy has been overturned. They watch in disbelieve as the horses buck loose and run free.

A

new day has come to befuddle the ancestor that speaks loudly. The ancestor that whispers of things hidden and recently discovered speaks now to those who can hear. It is the cycle of the bend in the road in space and in men. The old ancestor removes the hood from her head, eyes shining brightly, her mouth moving, the words coming swiftly gives the ordinances of the day: The name of god is HaHiYa, love god but do not fear him, as man and woman go hand in hand, be wise in what you believe is the truth, know right from wrong, joy and misery are arms on the same body, there are differences among men and men, women and women, and men and women, therefore we all require patience, peace is unstable, it must be protected, no man or government is greater than the Hidden One, people are not animals and are never to be treated as such, seek to be good, criminals soon grow weary of the chase.

The

ancestors speaks in whispers of things hidden and the children open their eyes. Someone asks them: whose child is this? And she answered: I am my old child, I have work to do I don't have time to play with you today. A generation of listeners to bring about the new day. One among them speaking words of wisdom leading them across a bridge into a new world as the old things pass away.

The

ancestor, speaking from a place beyond the rain, shows her back to the world and goes away. He has spoken all the words that the children can hear. More words than they can ever see in two thousand years. The ancestor spoke in words of things hidden and things recently discovered. Words for tomorrow, very little about today.

THE DAY OF SUBTRACTION

Those

who have awakened find themselves abandoning the old world. Smoke from the cities dance in the eyes of its inhabitants. Yesterday's sun unable to penetrate the veil of the new happiness. On a bridge sits a man with a double mind. Both his faces, the past and the present, peer into tomorrow trying to make an interpretation of things to come.

The

nite before several citizens came to his door to explain a problem. The woman first in line spoke first. She spoke of a husband, a man of misfortune in the hands of other men, his money gone. I gave her the five hundred dollars and she was gone. A man in his fifties told me of his troubled son. A son of dreams with a wife and two children and a mouth bigger than those who employed him. I gave him five hundred dollars and he was gone. Now looking up into my eyes the son of Kariel has come alone. The tears in his eyes spoke about the burden of sadness choking his heart. He opened his mouth and spoke these words: I do not have the five hundred dollars my mother owes. I don't have fifty dollars. My mother is dead. She was taken by a robber after she left this door. I will pay you this one dollar and nothing more. Kariel's lliving son gave me one dollar. I looked at him feeling his sadness and took the dollar, he walked quickly away. I looked at the man and woman still remaining. Something inside me was wrenching so I could do no more. Everybody understood and it ended last nite.

It

was strange. For forty years I had been doing this. From a hustler and other things. I had gave a man a dollar he brought me back two. I gave another man ten he brought me back fifteen. I gave a little girl some change on the way to school her mother brought me five dollars and a piece of cake and some chicken. Soon the word got around the neighborhood and I was in the lending business. Everybody started calling me Mayor. I was the Mayor of Central, the street on which I lived. Soon I had enough money to open a bar so I did. Policemen and politicians and thugs and prostitutes and gentlemen and ladies all came to my door. I was the pawnbroker of trading and a door that you could knock on when you needed help. In all the years of doing this I never told anybody to bring me anything more than what I had given. But always they brought me more. But the last few years the neighborhood had changed and an element of meanness had come down the street. Some nites when I heard the sounds of knocking I would pretend not to be home, turn the lights out or peep out the window. I had never felt fear before not in my own neighborhood. Talk was spreading that I had the big head or was upset because nobody had tried to help save my bar. I was glad it was gone. Glad that less people came to see me.

Something had happened to me. I wanted to spend time alone to understand myself and what my life was about. I never had a wife or children. In forty years it dawned on me one day I had never had a day off. I was all about business and time had eased by me. Now I wanted to have fun but found myself approaching sixty with a lot of empty memories.

I

was down at the lake and I saw these people, eight of them and they were listening to this young man with dreadlocks talking about coming into a new world, The Cry of Beauty. I could hear his words and he said the name of god was HaHiYa and that creation was a lliving language. He said many things that I had never heard before then he spoke of subtraction. He said that as one approaches god he begins to lose himself and that in losing himself he loses his friends and that in losing his friends he begins to lose his thoughts, all the things that he thought were true or important become less important and he finds himself choosing god instead. That he will come to a place where he is on a bridge. On this bridge he will discover his old face, his present face and on the other side of the bridge he will begin to see the glimpse of a new landscape, with new mountains and skies. The brilliant light of the sun shining there and the breath of air that is filled with a light fragrance. The word holiness abounds here released from the ball and chain of the old world.

This is the day of subtraction when the choice is made to take the steps across the bridge and fulfill the new heart's desire.

HaHiYa is waiting for your love.

I

sit here on a bridge of my own making. I turn my mind to what I had done with my life. My old face sees the old days that can't be reclaimed. I remember Betty, I remember Rock and Black Mack, and Little Ron and Way Way. Dead. Places burned down or torn down replaced by new buildings. A new generation of people with their own ideas and the passing away of many things. And I think about what the young man with dreadlocks said: the face of creation does not change it only becomes brighter to those who have become its witness. The traffic between men and women does not change it only leads to entanglement. The day when we have had enough of entanglement is the day we begin to seek a way out. The bridge of the day of subtraction starts construction deep within yourself. Every step thereafter is on that bridge until you cross over to the over side. He said his name is Seso and that you will find me waiting there with the true word of love,

The Cry of Beauty and the spirit of HaHiYa holding all of creation together.

I am standing up on my own bridge and making my way across to the other side. The sound of a river flows in my head and the blue sky is filled with stars. A bright light shines down and looking to my left and to right I see thousands of bridges appearing with others like myself crossing over. I hear the sound of music and I am greeted by well-wishers who hold my hand and guide me in to this new happiness. The Beauty of wisdom embraces me and the symbol of love, my heart, takes flight. And in the midst, I see the man who called himself Seso with his hands reaching out for us all. On the other side of the bridge I have crossed I see a multitude of angry faces with their fist raised and they are throwing things and cursing and their faces all full of tears. Those of us who have crossed over look at them knowing that they will not come. Their faces belong to the old world, they will not accept anything more. I turn and join the others. This plain rises steadily into the mountains in the distance. I hear the singing of hundreds beyond me calling us to climb even higher, cross this mountain and enter a valley of wonder on the other side.

TRANSFIGURATION

Looking

to the left and to the right shadows appear. Not solid things.

It is the present world going in slow motion. A click on the reel of time framed with the intentions of those who lead. They give each other credentials, the evidence of their power, a mandate to lead. They make the people submit to what they call the real thing, life as they are inventing it. Not allowing or permitting a new face to surface from the crowd or approach the crown usurped on their heads.

Looking

to the left and to the right shadows appear. The face of one who questions right and wrong. The face of another that wonders out loud why so many are poor and feel pain. The voice of a woman muffled by the fist of a lost soul. Children who stun us with their bright minds and unusual tongues put in the fog of uniformity, fall into conformity or rebel without being able to identify specifically who is at fault. These shadows gather and then disperse raising the clamor for change. Their mission stuck in the air of nonsolid politics condemned by generalities of the norm and predetermined strategies of disenfranchisement. Understanding that shadows don't have the means to wage protracted political struggles against the soulless giant presented as the obstacle to block all attempts of change.

Yet,

on the fringes of the wizardry, electronic megalopolis, the birth of an unexpectant warrior has occurred. The weight of oppression squeezing the inner life, pressing down the old form into a new form fit to survive the human holocaust of the modern world. The weight of the oppression pressing out the shadow until it speaks through the sheer force of rebellion against atrocity. Slowly a form takes shape talking to itself as it witnesses millions in trouble. Seeing no way out trapped in a fire ring of deception and lies. The furnace of industrial might cooking living souls without blinking an eye. Pillaging the earth and pushing production through a revolving door leading from the front door of one country through the backdoor of another. The policy towards the Latins reversed against the Asians, corrupted against the Abukan and homogenized with deadly results against the Indians home and abroad. Exporting the idea of help and commonality and exiting with bags of money, leaving behind tricky politics.

The

warrior that nobody expected squeezed from the heart of hopelessness stands up to begin a messianic mission. Proclaiming a new god, HaHiYa, and a new book, The Cry of Beauty to make things right. On what road will the doers of hurt meet him. And when they meet this One how much fear will they bring to conquer him who comes only armed with the glory of love and peace.

THE DEAD

It

is good. That is how the creation began. Good. Goodness and mercy. It was spoken according to the beginning of all things. The light separating from the womb of darkness journeying forth as the prodigal never to return to the point of the essence.

I

saw a field filled with the objects of time. Suns, moons, water, earth, mountains and valleys, fishes, animals, trees, flowers, and man. It was good according to the will of the Creator, unknowable, unreachable, the teacher of all that beheld itself, of all that came to know itself as separate parts bound to the whole. This goodness touching all with the endless lessons of how to be good. The witness, The Cry of Beauty, with its voice crying in the wilderness of the lost beckoning those that have gone astray to come home, to enlist once again in the fold. What can be said to doers of those who have gone astray attempting to make a creation of their own. What name can be given to their idea of goodness that leads many into the valleys of nails. Nineteen nails nailed into their bodies. Planks on a ship set adrift on a sea made by their tears. The rain of hard labor flooding the embankments of a river of deceit. Come down with me past the figures of time that have left their mark jotted down on the pages of history and remember the blood as it eddies among the bodies of the deceased rotting outside the doors of the heads of state. The thorns of lies chills under the setting sun picked at by birds falling from their perch upon the innocent whose only crime was opening their mouths in protest because they knew goodness did not walk by and extend a helping hand.

I

see a field filled with red flowers, roses, carnations, and white tulips. Blood on the ground from a tree whose generations unfold as black leaves. Nurturing the roots admired by the men and women of honor and love and trust and obedience. I bend my head knowing that many had no choice because of the bondage placed upon the ancestors and the ancestor's children. The voice of goodness echoing in the shadows: how long will the ignorant survive?

The

dead must now stand up. Come out of the caves of doubt and watch as a spring of water escapes the stones erupting on the mountain top. There is a figure of Beauty dancing in the morning twilight. Singing a song of salvation that makes the whole world stand still and wonder. There is a figure of Beauty carrying a sword of transfiguration raised to be good with The Book of The

Ocmaba in both his hand. Speaking in a firm voice. Holding the flowers of gentleness close to his heart in answer to those that have led millions into the valley of deception.

The
war of neglect begun by the fathers of dirt is being turned into mud by the waters of the true spirit flowing down from the mountainside. Bones that were stones clothe themselves by the Trees of Light and the rain of love falls from the sky of hope.

If
you cannot see this, if you cannot feel this then the time of the beginnings and all that the beginning spoke then count yourself among those who do not know the specter of light.

HaHiYa has raised one of His own. Gathered the thoughts of this One to reproduce the original sound. All that I have made I made good, none of this is dead. It is only becoming what I envisioned at the beginning. If there is another creation made by men I know not its name. It is a wanderer full of dark flames and schemes to be, in time, set aside with the rest of the dead. The word of HaHiYa is alive and moves among the lliving. It raises the stolen to their proper place and gives them a perspective of the rays of light. It opens the well and fills the buckets they draw forth with a divine destiny. To know this water is not to know thirst. Fill your cups and drink with me.

THE EMPTY TOMB

Lift
your heads and proclaim the day of salvation has removed the stone. All those whom you thought, the sons and daughters of HaHiYa's children were dead and dying, have been raised to a new life. The tomb is empty. Visitors to the grave come as men who faces turn ashy white for the body is not present. They brought a light into the dark place where for over four hundred years we had borne suffering are too late. HaHiYa has sent word for us to get up and accept the offering of the lliving. Think not that the fallen were not kept in a book of records. The mood of the masters has changed greatly as they search in vain for the footsteps of the newly departed.

She
was a woman of a small beginning. Her voice wailing long into the nite. Her feet spread by the burden of the beast placed upon her back. The men she loved beaten until they spoke in foreign tongues. A foreign fire upon her lips forced to receive objects of gratification.

HaHiYa heard her tears as they fell like lead to the earth. Heavy tears because her sons face was caked with blood. Heavy tears because she heard the neck of one of her children breaking. Later that same nite a white snake came to visit her.

She produced a litter of children holding back a giant tear of shame festering in her soul. One day by the river she saw the image of a man handing her a seed. She dropped the seed in the river. Every day for thirty-nine days she came to the river and prayed:

help me with this burden

I carry a strange beast on my back

his legs upon mine

his arms around me

his tongue sticking in my ear

feeding me bloody meat

harvesting his corn

drinking his wine

showing my children his wonders

slipping into another century a bag of tricks

to continue an act of unspeakable fantasy

send me your word of peace to unarm this

beast from my thoughts…

On

the fortieth day the seed sprouted. She watched all day as it grew into a man with dreadful hair to lock out the past. He spoke to her. His mouth a black cave produced a single flame with a book at the end of it. He spit the book on the ground and she reached for it. He said wait before placing your hand upon it. Pass it on to your child he will know what to do with it. It was in the cool of the morning when she came back for the book. The man was sleeping by the shore but the book was covered with a seal, a nine pointed shape. Her footsteps aroused the sleeping man whose face had changed greatly. He was shining when she lay with him. She gave birth to nine souls, each with their own generation. The first child was Wint, one foot there and one foot here, he walked awkwardly all his life. Then came Mo, a sufferer of long days. Lolly came next, a pop of a female, bearer of a field of speckled lilies. These three came before her and were like little pebbles tossed into the nite. She saw her own face and the faces of the five to follow. Sweet Nite

was a lovely babe, then came the Turtle with her brood of twelve. Out of her inner self a light began and falling from a womb came a wound of blood, the mighty Tur, thought to be an error, a gatherer of sound. After him came Kabib, one who tied himself to a vine producing a heady

wine. Kabib, the father of crafts and measurements, and the star of the north who carried the seed of Zun, the owner of the book of promise. He filled her womb with a hidden word. Then he said he would return in time. Her eyes were closed and she felt a gentle touch upon her cheek and his voice said we have brought this for your children. Then he made a hole in a nearby tree, she handed him the book and he placed the book in the small place and covered it with the fire from his mouth. Your child will know when it is time. He will speak when the nite is at its darkest hour. In his day the Mussii will show its face.

Now

the hour has passed. The beast that was upon her back lays on its back kicking the air. What has been done to you? one of the masters is heard asking. The beast begs for gold before he will speak. Why should we who made you pay you to tell us what we want to know. Because you don't know the answer, the beast responds. How long did you think I could hold on when she was sweating so? Tell us who removed the stone and where did the people go? The beast looked surprised, there were never any bodies there, only a dark blank space. I sat upon her back because everything had been removed. It was her children coming day after day. Each with its own generation and they supplied her with questions. She began to torment herself looking into the dust of her past. One day she caught a glimpse of me washing herself in the river. Turning around quickly no one was to be found as I sat on her back with my hands on her head and my lips sealed to her ears. Her legs were so sweaty I lost my grip and climbed higher. Her children observed her legs were straighter and she stood taller than before. Later that night her dreams came swiftly and she saw herself flying through the sky. The sun was beginning to rise still she slept, dreaming of flying. Her children gathered around the bed shaking her but she was dreaming of flying, of being free and she was sweating from the excitement, sweating like never before. When she had been ill the sweat was sticky and I could clamp down even more. This sweat of freedom was slippery. It put pictures on her blankness, her mind began to fill its own reservoir with buckets of words, she mumbled in her sleep. The children were agitated and began to beat upon her to wake her. I slipped from her oily body to the floor. The trampling children stampeded me, vexing my soul and when she opened her eyes she saw me, a beast on the floor. She placed her children under her arms and ran out the door. Taking them to the river they all prayed:

I want to go home
open the door
it has been so many years
they laid me in a tomb
didn't even cry over me
said I was not even human
just a working thing
just somebody to ignore
have me when you want me
then push me out the door
pregnant with days and nites of darkness
too tired to scrub my own floor
I did everything for my children
hoping to stay alive
just long enough to be a witness
to the coming glory
A child of mine to build a house of glory
we all can call home

This is all I have to tell you masters. The tomb is empty. The stone was a name you placed in front of it has been removed. I will accept your money, I am a beast designed for ruin. What name will you now call upon to hold her and her children. They will no longer serve your god. They have found one of their own.

HaHiYa loves them and will receive them all in his new home. Do you judge yourselves on a coin spinning around on heads or tails or do you sit it on the edge and see it as a circle, a moon reflecting the light of the father sun, the real old story of wisdom unchanged for as long as the heavens spin overhead. I am also the same beast, the red dragon covering a fourth of the heavens until my cycle is done. A bloody thing to be led to be circumcised from the heart. I know that soon or late I will be undone. But what of you men in high places who will you serve or are you the real men struggling in the tomb, making noise because you can't find your way out.

A

great voice is rising above the din of the setting sun. I see her coming down the road and she is carrying a great book overflowing with the words of the people of her nation. A bright smile on the faces of her children. Even the old people of her tribe have a cherry appearance. The salvation so long promised has come to be. On the floor in the tomb of bondage scattered bandages and the smell of healing ointments lay in a corner. Wind brings dust to cover the bloodstains left by tired feet. The bed sheet has been removed and the mattress set on fire.

A cup from which the thirsty drank survival removed by an unknown hand and a set of keys with their locks lay on a hillside bent and twisted. All evidence that any soul was ever present in the tomb has been removed or destroyed. Not one thought remains.

The

joyous music of the free, of the risen bends its way through the trees and can be clearly heard in the valley. Cascading from the mountain top to the river below. Not a single soul is quiet but speaks eloquently of the work of HaHiYa.

We

stand here with hearts on fire

fingertips tingling

the dreadfulness of our hair falling freely

we open our mouths

offer the holiest prayer of thanksgiving

the power of HaHiYa burning the air

Star of wonder singing praises

walking beside us showing us the way

emerging from a blank wall of darkness

passing from the cave and receiving a bouquet of flowers

a kiss of divine love

the word of eternal peace

thank god HaHiYa at last we are truly free

HaHiYa is here to guide us

with laws of peace and prosperity

we climb into his mountain of love and

an abode of everlasting tranquility

peace and peace and peace and peace and peace

HaHiYa (the hand of life)

1. Where, in the time of men, is it written than man knows the works of god or even my name unless I raise a servant to speak it.

2. I have placed my witnesses among men, in their capital places and among the lowest who till the soil. Giving one to be over another and on streets as neighbors one to another to sow seeds for times to come.

3. I have placed upon their heads my character that I might know them in the day of coming forth.

4. Now the swift hour of ascension of my flower flies to the world and some stare as if blind. By my hand was the whole earth set upon itself, shifting left to right bringing men face to face.

5. Set the place of the eyes on distant shores where my chosen suffer. I will make man anew. My chosen walk as if crippled, despised by mankind they bicker amongst themselves for the wound is deep in a hallow place near the heart.

6. In due time I will set a fire in their souls to awaken them from a hellish world they have come to know. All men will know my hand is upon their shoulder and that I am the guide under the soles of their women's feet. I will be a comfort to them and a judge and they will live their days in my bosom.

7. Man made them naked and shortened their years with the affliction of hard labor and neglect. But I will come with a quiet rain to soothe their aching backs. I will give them the water of life so that their thoughts will not faint or fall away. These are my people bearing the pain of feeling alone and abused in the world. Those who call themselves master are called upon to give an account of what they have done to the treasure of my heart.

8. The measure of my Creation is balanced on the scales. Woe to the position holders who have acted as the final judge over those sent by me under the cover of servants. Did you not think there was a message revealed in my book? The dog is taught to guard the sheep and guide them on the path not set upon them with fangs and cunning leading them astray. Is the fox or other beast to blame if the dog pretends to be lame?

9. See the morning creation arise, it is I, HaHiYa. I change my face repeatedly so that you will never know which day I have chosen to come to see about mine. I call my most trusted by name and he steps forward. He brings me the bones of those that ache and have cried for me and place them in my hand. And when they see me they rejoice and call me my by name. HaHiYa

I hear them and let them know they are my people, welcome home, sit down while I close this door. I have much to reveal to my loved ones.

HORSES WITH EYES

HaHiYa

my God and my salvation how can I pay tribute to the wisdom you impart to me. A tiny edge of your vision comes and rests upon my shoulder, whispers like the wind across the hairs on my chin and then raises up to fill my eyes with wonders I never imagined.

The

beauty of one of your days rises calmly. How are we to know that because a few clouds gather on the horizon a terrible storm is brewing out of our sight. That a ship laden with humans would be made into beast of burden. That a rider of horrors buckled with a sword in his hand would cut off the heads of people. Blight them with the deadliest disease of all, ignorance of themselves. Climb upon their backs until their knees buckled, riding them about on their hands and knees until they only knew themselves as animals in a field without land of their own. Set free in this state of wildness to wander around drinking from the springs of another man's cup. I saw in a vision the cup being emptied and thrown into the trash. From what cup now will these people who were made into animal's drink?

    HaHiYa

those who have permission have been admitted into this circle and come to you with open arms. We receive the bounty of your endless grace and loving calmness.

The

rider of the horse has been unseated and looks into space amazed at the new circumstance. The offspring of the horse wearied of wandering and took for themselves leaves of the trees instead of the grass of the field. Raising their heads and hoofs. Seeing for the first time in many generations hands instead of feet, walking upright, a new position to behold all around themselves.

I saw the one who made the many raise their heads. Upon his body and head were many seeping wounds and holes but the eye of this one beheld a vision of beauty in a tree on a distant plateau. Climbing up a unmarked rocky path this one parted the way and came upon a pond of sweet water from which the tree was fed. Boldly entering in he heard a voice murmuring in the water and felt a cool breeze blowing across his soul. After many days he returned walking upright and all were amazed and when the master, who was his rider, beat him none said a word but turned away in shyness and fear for the wrong thing had been done. Again, this one went to the place of calmness walking upright. One day upon his return he spoke, something that had never been done before.

I

have been to a place of calmness. There is a wind there that warms my soul. There is a pond of the sweetest water and from it there is a voice that murmurs. I believe it is the voice of my ancestor, the voice of one much older and wiser than any I have ever known. I sit in peace and listen and my eyes are filled with visions. I see us walking like the ones who rode us. I walk and know now that this is the way we all should be. If you are afraid because of the wounds you see on me I will take you to the plateau, up there and you will see a different me.

There

were many that day that believed. When they returned all of them were walking not one could be found who was upon his hands and knees. These old people, who had been made into horses and beast of burden, were youthful and displayed a beauty all could see. Each had a leaf from the tree they carried in their hands, slowly chewing upon it in a hollow place in the mouth.

HaHiYa

I know that this thing that was done was done by your hand. All those who believed became knowers of what gifts you had laid in storage for this special day.

If

there are any of you who still think you are horses or beast of burden to be ridden then I invite you to come with me to the sweetest pond and listen to the voice in it murmuring, feel the cool wind blow warmly across your soul, taste a leaf from the tree on top of this plateau. If you are not afraid then hold your head up, look through my wounds and scars and see the real me, filled with the Creator's holy beauty and calmness, and tell me you have no desire to be free.

    peace and peace and peace

COME

I

look out upon a hill of humans with weapons in their hands, their tongues sharp tools flinging words boiling with splitting blistering. A wall built by the unforgiving. Men and women separating themselves into temples of loneliness and fear. Sadness draped over the clouds. Deceived by the work of false men announcing the setting sun of Armageddon, abominations and the hordes of horrors riding pale horses in a night of unbelievable darkness and terror.

A

true note of glorious music lines the shore. Born in spiritual waters it rises without the permission of any man. Born in the heart of the risen one it takes refuge in a holy consciousness seeking a field of bones tossed aside to lay its seed. Sprouting in the dead of winter while the others sleep. And when the first signs of spring arrive, it moves out of the ground into a shadow, assuming the position of one that has traveled through the ages on the road of truth out of sight of men who claim to know.

I

send these words out to the world. Who allowed this much sadness to come into HaHiYa's creation. So unmindful of its endless Beauty. Beauty that let its tears flow in the light. A lliving rainbow containing all things in its rivers of glory. HaHiYa forgive us all.

We

are coming. We do hear the sound of your voice calling in the night of the wind of revelation. And when we arrive we come with palms washed and our tongues rounded by the words peace and peace and peace. Soljahs of HaHiYa's army to straighten what was wrong and passed out to believers as the word to make men one.

THE GOOD BOOK

Where

are the people, the sons and daughters of my tribe of soljahs. Where is the one son and the daughter that have claimed HaHiYa as their god? They have hidden themselves in the red stones, the bluecoats of animal skins or the wood in ancient trees. Have they buried themselves in the sands of time, covering themselves in veils of mysteries that are empty mazes from the imagination of men who pretended to know the difference between the light and the truth.

When

the lliving came into being they were no more than flower's, petals spinning in the winds of creation. Yet, bye and bye, the word came to them in the form of fire, the first mystical dance. Counting the bones under the skin of animals they knew another aspect of the magic of creation. For the hand of man was a tool and the bones and stones lying about became instruments of advancement. What the eyes beheld became subjects to change, bent to the will of the tribe, and later to the individual. The sound of men and women building, sounds of human magic. What they could think to do they found in the earth the things to do it with.

How

then with what has been found to be useful did men stray into the lakes of misery? Even the long horse with its many riders cannot stay the tides of waste coming ashore, the water purple and dark. This was the same horse upon whose back rode all the children of the mother of Wint, whose foot was here and there. And now is the time of the book held in secret by Zun, in the city of Zantioch. Replacing the empty tomb with words carried in the heart of Seso. The book whose pages were blank have the markings of the word in the life of Seso and all those with him. And were all that was known revealed no man could read the endless symbols placed there. Give to them a portion of the Good Book.

The

son and daughter of the tribe sits down, no longer hiding themselves from the moment of revelation. Placing their hands in the open, submitting to what would be for them wisdom they had not known.

Son

your father has need of you, your hands and your heart to locate stones of the lliving. Place them in order according to the age of the cycle. Each stone must be of the proper form and weight, decreasing as the son increases. Time ending at one past midnight. Time beginning when the sun marries the daughter waiting at the crossroads of east and west. Watch the winged ones raise the northern standard and southern home of the double six. All these things spoken of in the old tradition now waning on the broken fence of the rising moon. Symbols of the night spoken in whispers, men of renown kept in secret. HaHiYa releasing the light of truth for the new day, embarking on the waters of an ocean of sweet water, the waves taking many out to sea to see the new horizon.

Daughter

take the hand of the old one as she walks by. The dust on her trail the result of being close to the ground. Mothers feel the earth. The blood seeping from their womb, speaking with a voice that seems never to grow old or tired. The old one, the original ancestor going to a place of retirement. Known even before the Bull, her eye filling the halls of all that her husband beheld. Queen of the river of thoughts sitting now in a bay, silent because time has wound around her like thick mud. Before she goes she tells all to the new daughter. Oh, how sweet the sound of young laughter feeling for the first time wisdom rising like a serpent in her consciousness. She knows what she must do.

The

son and daughter rise together before the tribe in a moment of acceptance. The king and queen of the next moment and all that each second would become. For in the new day the union of male and female will be fulfilled and the word will proceed from both as if spoken in one voice.

The witness, time, shows them the cup and from its bowl they drink deeply. The wine of pretty red colors and the taste of bitter attributes reaches their lips and they know the early lesson of wisdom. The face of the morning, of the sun of glory and the fall of the evening stars with their symbols of warning and the cunning wit of the men of betrayal.

Can

man only witness the beauty and not be inspired to truth, to goodness. The message opens the day, beauty and hope, a new table of bountifulness spread out under the clouds, where the light of the sun shines through. Making colors the most wondrous of things possible. Inspiring the imagination of mankind to duplicate what he sees in creation, to copy the wonders, bend all that he sees to his own manipulation. How is it that men think they can fly if not the original creation? Making it possible for human consciousness to delve into the well of the unknown without a messenger, the faith of inspiration, his vision a companion. The creation an ark of forms yet unknown journeys to be discovered. And in this new time the witness will go far, even among the stars because it is his heart's desire. Is this not magic? Does not creation provide the unwritten formulae? And when men arrive to the new places will there not be more that he has not thought to know? All this and more, ancient dust to the creator, the unknowable. Know then the good given to you is all that you can know.

Be good. The sons and daughters of all the tribes are admonished to be good. Apply this admonishment to yourselves. Let not the vanity of age or learning lead you to consider an escape route or handoff to another. None are too busy to see their own work. Nor be amazed when things fall against you, the grain of your season spoiled by an invasion of beetles burrowing in from the bottom out of sight. The sight of your eye handicapped by selfglory and position after a life of work undone by a poor man's son. There the balance of life becomes the witness and makes the adjustments. Life does not ask for permission to adjust itself, it goes about its business and never says a word good or bad. Men and women swear at the undone thing, as if it were alive, and it is, but it has not a body or feelings yet it is as accurate as the hour of the day. It does not pretend that it does not exist yet lessons abound for all, both animal and human and it turns not its head around to count the casualties or the righteous. The book of the good goes through each day tirelessly. Make the decisions of your own doings and pray that when you turn down that road it is the one full of flowers and not ravenous things to rip and tear at you.

Say to yourself as you would say to your children be good, we all know the difference between good and evil.

ZANTIOCH

There

is a stranger at the gate where the sun sets. He says his name is Omad Zand. There is blood on his cheek and his heels are swollen.

His

lips are dry and he says that his back is weary from too much searching. He says he has been searching for the land where men do not throw stones at one another and women cast the shadow of love when they pass by. He has been placed in the shade of the inner wall and given water and fruit to refresh himself.

We

stand before you Omad, Ruh and Ova. Do you know the name of the place where you set your feet? This is Zantioch, the door to civilization.

Zand: I have come from the place where men throw stones of all sizes
      upon one another.

Ruh: Civilization is not the opportunity under the disguise of freedom to throw stones. That is
      not the beginning point, it is the signal of the end.

Zand: There were so many heads in the government with lines leading back to
      merchants lies made knots around truth.

Ova: Form itself is orderly division when properly applied.

Zand: I closed my eyes repeatedly, searching my soul for answers and
      always I came upon a blank wall. That is until today. This morning
      I saw a blue light resting on the horizon. I never took my eye from it.
      It was the quietest I had ever been.
      I saw this place, a city, and then a gate with pillars facing the sun as it set. But I didn't see
      a floor or roadway or streets

Ruh: The citizen is Zantioch. He has come to the way of civilization.
      He has come to know stillness.
      He has come to know this because of what he and others
      created. To be civilized is to know peace in the land.
      To journey from city to city in common with other citizens.
      Animals of prey lie in wait to subdue their common enemy.
      Citizens are not animals and lie in wait for no one.

Ova: The guiding principles of civilization are truth, will, love and submission to peace. Truth begins with the Day of Subtraction. Will is the discipline to stay the course of truth. Love is the witness that sees the glory of creation and willingly submits to HaHiYa because there he will find wisdom

Ruh: We are the protectors of Zantioch, the guardians of Citizen. No man could have told you of this place. Only in your soul could you come upon us. The steps we take do not leave footprints. Open the gate and look out and reveal to us what you see.

Omad looked out into a vast emptiness. No sky, no ground, no wind, sun, no animals, only a deep mystifying silence. Turning around he looked upon Zantioch and saw the principles as forms making cities whose streets led to fountains of truth and he watched as the truth became will and will became love and love submitted to HaHiYa. Outside the city were mountains of stones of all sizes that men had laid aside and he saw the robes of peace that they had adorned themselves with.

Omad: I have spent many days searching for this place and now I am home.

Ova: Omad this is only the beginning. We have much to teach you. This robe is new and fits all who have just begun to return to civilization. Enter with us and accept the way of peace of HaHiYa's The Cry of Beauty.

THE APPEAL

When
we approach men with the revelations we have received what are the words we are to use that will not seem rebellious. What is there in an appeal that can be seen as honorable and just without taking a step backward or viewed as controversial or adversarial. Those who have suffered long and have been turned into beast of burden and objects of derision see the light of a new day. They see the day of inner peace and solvency. The waters of life having washed away all that they have known until they stand naked before mankind with an appeal in their hand that they are no longer the subject of oppression of any man or nation. The subject of salvation has been placed on the mantle of their consciousness and it has come from within.

The
signer of this appeal is HaHiYa, the god of this people. This speaker trades his words in the form of a vision raising witness after witness that the day of revelation has come. The warners of the past generations have come and gone. The fruit of the flowers has ripened and can no longer be denied as they fall from the hanging trees where their forefathers were held against their will. The times of suffering when the hands of hope were slapped away seeking a crust of bread or a place to lay their head, kneeling in the woods among the trees praying to god for mercy and to soften the heart of those who hurt them, who hurt us all.

A
few who came close to the eyes of pain walked away shivering, mixing a strong drink to increase their forgetfulness, living in a place of denial while the machinery of pain continued to rip out the guts of another human. In a land where the heart is dry many feel the pain and succumb prematurely because of the wounds of shame.

The
appeal now lies on the table, an obvious thorn plucked from the feet of millions. The trail of blood a shadow on the road to freedom. The children of the children of the children march unfettered toward the land of promise and their god HaHiYa leads them with a shining light.

The
writing of the appeal clearly marked in the mind of the awakened.

I serve no god but HaHiYa

I am his messenger

I am the ambassador of the assignment of liberation

I will speak the words of wisdom

I will know peace among the tribes of my people

I will walk the road of joy

I will take the words of the Cry of Beauty with me daily

I submit to the partnership of men and women

I submit to the partnership of mankind none above the other

I will not turn my back to those who have counseled against me and act in enmity

I or those who represent me will make note of my life and my actions, my health and my dealings with men and women as a record so that goodness becomes the pathway of life. Is it not the duty of men to keep the standard of life standing as erect as the day before and not let life fall into disarray or dismay?

We who have suffered know too well the many tributaries of pain when life has been led astray

I submit myself to the daily duties of cleanliness and self-government

These obligations are of a personal nature and are not the province of dogmatism. How much more is required of men to reflect what is evident in the creation about him-beauty of person beauty of mind and beauty of soul.

Fairness in commerce and social exchange so that none fear loss but if one is subjected to loss then they have the human right to seek correction.

Those who seek to unbalance the scales are the creators of rebellion.

If a man does not have these obligations as a natural part of his being then that person is on the road of those who do not understand the beauty of HaHiYa's creation and are seeking to make a creation of their own.

HaHiYa's

appeal is a home deep in the heart of his beloved. Sit quietly and observe this creation and its wisdom will in time reveal itself to you. It is a stone of enduring light and benevolence, resolute and constant.

Those

that lead oppression listen to this appeal. It is the day of release. It is written on the heart and spoken to the consciousness and witnessed in the soul. It is clear and there is no substitute. In the clouds HaHiYa has signed his signature and on the trees and on the stars, in the water and on the animals and on you. There will be a day of peace in the soul of this people or there will be suffering more than you can know.

THE FLAME OF HAHIYA

When
they see the fire of HaHiYa walking by they speak in whispers, throwing words at the background of things that make his life. They say who spoke to him and told him he was the One to come? Did anyone see him under a tree talking to any men or women about the promise of things to be? There are no mountains or caves in this place, no wise men following any type of sun or another who spoke of his coming. None of us, who are recognized by our works, have had anything to do with him. Haven't we heard that even among those who knew him as a child no one noticed anything special about him. Members of his family look upon him with sympathy and said they did not know the nature or source of his influence that led him onto the path he walks. They said only that for a number of years he worked quietly and then he seemed to be moving, almost imperceptibly into this position of recognition. Yet, how are we to believe when the abundance we look for is not evident?

The
flame of HaHiYa has received his inheritance. Those who speak have not received the light that opens eyes. The light of HaHiYa comes to whom HaHiYa wills, working from within on the mountain of the soul, in a cave of divine consciousness where wisdom resides. Entering into the heart it begins as a spark ignited by the desire to know more. The branches of wisdom coming with time, each experience a log placed upon the campsite where patience and trust sit as true guides. Questions from the human mind fade from view as evidence of the divine presence rises higher and higher, the horizon tilts and all things point to the zenith of the inner being. A straight line of oneness directly from within the divine to the heart, lighting the eternal flame of love and understanding, the flame of HaHiYa.

Those
looking upon HaHiYa's Flame will only see the background, the circumstances of life as they unfold naturally in the outer world. They will see the passage of time, one year, five years, ten years, twenty years, thirty years and will speak only of what they see, the outer man and his accomplishments. And they will judge themselves wise as they look upon the hill of human achievements and where they might stand, they will judge where others might stand and they will measure this one that men and women have begun to claim because of his spiritual presence. They will sit at the table pretending to be powerful men with paper documents, make exchanges and deals to further control the outcome of men's lives. They will go about making speeches and

receiving applause. Be treated with pleasures and monies, with embroidered invitations sent to their doors because representatives from the nations houses of commerce and politics want to talk with them.

Who

are they to question or doubt if a man comes out of the midst of things, saying things they have never heard before and proclaim this one a charlatan, a hustler, and a liar. Those that come to the chair of recognition by natural selection, sat down there by his neighbors or others who heard his word, who did not ask for the seat that others have claimed as theirs by right of possession, taking it upon themselves to declare who belongs to what, seeing to it that the stage is set before anybody gets there has become the moral dilemma of their own making.

The

flame of HaHiYa has grown from within until its light can do nothing but shine. Burning away the earthly desires, nothing remains even of the ashes. Like the Empty Tomb no evidence remains that anyone ever lived there, the space filled with fire without dimensions. The fire of abundance given while yet he lives in this world. The true inheritance of a witness that has stepped out of the shade into the light of wisdom and acceptance. It is no wonder when this one speaks, all those near listen. There could not have been one to announce the coming of this one, it was a consequence of life being squeezed on all levels, a flower emerging through stone watered by a festering call of tired men and women lost in a valley of measurements, fed traditions that are diseases of life created by greedy men. Stuck in books with false revelations based on the motion of the sun and the moon. Did they not think that one day all that they have done would not be exposed even if it took five thousand years to arrive at the day of Armageddon, the day when the original consciousness of wisdom would return to claim all those that are His.

All

those who have looked upon the back of the carrier of the Flame of HaHiYa, did not really look closely, did not see what had transpired within. They did not know that he had arrived at the road where earthly conditions cease and that he had stepped on to the road where spiritual evidence begins. They could not have known that his glance rose above the traffic of human noise and chatter and bantering. That his only interest was to be a guide and that his desire was to share the peace proclaiming itself daily in his heart. They could not have known that he no longer was just the outer man that anyone could see but he had combined his inner self to his heart and mind and become one straight line of divine energy and love attached like an umbilical cord to HaHiYa.

That
he received hourly nourishment and was always refreshed. That what man spoke about of as abundance would soon fade away, disappearing into the hands of their grandchildren, the original vision of their concept an old coupon yellowed by time. Unlike the eternal flame of HaHiYa whose light increases with the passage of each day. Many coming in a later day to witness this revelation seeing for themselves the new world of abundance. The plan revealed to them within their own heart and their own inner self on a mountain of spiritual consciousness, in a cave where wisdom resides. Looking over into a crevice on their left where all the old traditions of pain and restriction had been trampled upon and placed. Entering the transfigured world of men and women sitting at the same table of government, commerce and spiritual belief. Know that the human family has emerged from all those things labeled as mystery and mystery has been removed. Trusting in the benevolence of HaHiYa's word, attending the campsite where the flame is light, placing the logs of life's experience on the fire one by one, gleaning the wisdom from each. Using patience and trust in a higher consciousness. Stepping away from the *what we know* to be wrong and going always in the direction of the light. Working on this path until we step off the road of earthly conditions and on to the road of spiritual evidence while yet we live in this world. To become what god had intended. What book do you need to read or what person do you need to listen too to tell you to be good? Why do men say that this or that is complicated when they know that if they cease being bad or greedy or angry or jealous or possessive it is easy to find the pathway of goodness and wisdom and not treachery and deception. What apple tree in HaHiYa's creation has ever denied any man the freedom to walk up and take its fruit? Is it that men call themselves wise and do not know that each of us has fruit to share and that men and women have a right to it freely without conditions? When did men forget that we are not our makers? We are created by the will and grace and mercy of HaHiYa. That all that we do is a book revealing who we are and what we have done?
If
HaHiYa is gracious enough to raise as many as he chooses and yet we question it even though we can see the divine glory in the word and works and the only confusion is that he was not one that anyone recognized because he had not spoken before? What is the nature of this arrogance that says when HaHiYa sends one of his own there is an announcement? What is the nature of this tradition and when did it really begin and why was a lamb combined with a fish on a man who left no footprints of his existence?
The
Flame of HaHiYa burns eternally. It is the generator that drives the heart and soul. It is the voice

of peace and wisdom. It requires nothing to exist. It requires no one to speak. It is the abundance of HaHiYa that he offers. It is the fruit of his divine tree. It never reveals itself to the untried and can only be found in the recesses of the cave of divine wisdom. Its light sits quietly at a campfire where you place the logs of experience for examination and revelation until you reach the place where the road suddenly ends. If you decide to step across into the new horizon you cannot return to the old world, it disappears immediately and you are now on the journey to divine wisdom and goodness led by your patience and trust. Know that the revelation and realization of peace exist in this world. That you may enjoy the fruits of their abundance while yet you live. That the traditions of men are doomed to be discarded along with all the other physical elements but the treasures of HaHiYa are eternal and never spoil no matter how long you leave them in the light of the sun. All those things which are his only get brighter.

REVELATIONS

The true revelation of creation is its constant existence. All men that exist in the galaxies come to her womb and are given life. They proceed as a seed into a vine whose roots seem to sprout in air for life has not a tenuous cord binding it to any particular place. Men bow before the immeasurable distance of creation and even sit with open mouths as the beauty of sandy beaches are touched by the waters of the seas and the sun and moon rise and set in skies burning with the desire to do more than they did yesterday.

What kind of mystery exists that permits men to rob from one another and plunder neighbors taking from the human concept of freedom and choice? Is there any man who thinks that a forced existence will go unpunished? The scroll of events is flying even as this is revealed to you. No man can run around the corner or cross into a nearby galaxy to escape the deed done to subdue another. A transgression is a transgression. It has a season of maturity coming.

The light of eternity goes not out. It cannot be sealed nor has it ever been sealed but to those who have twisted the message by putting wisdom into a briar patch of useless symbols and rituals the constant quiet of wisdom stands unmoved as its candidate's step into the choir of its song and learn the words written there without the help of any book known to man. Revelations written in spaces between atoms connecting the material world and the spiritual world. The same day dawning over and over its voice high and low, swinging without moving, moving without swinging, all things at once melting the ice of ignorance seeming to cover the eyes of those made blind by men who suffer. The ants have come to claim their dead to take them back to a civilization familiar to them.

The earth has eyes and it is watching all that men do and it is preparing a response that will be long remembered by those that live on.

BOOK OF THORNS

Illuminate

a tree in darkness with the moons light and behold the mind of men.

The

prophet is the tree rising at dawn bathing in the glory of the morning sun.

When

the people come the prophet spills a little of his vision on a spoon from which the thirsty may sip.

Open

the Book of Splendor given in cycles of silence then the eye can be opened.

The

cleanliness of the prophet is a river to wash away the grime clinging to the soul. He is a strong man holding the weight of many seasons in his mind like a sweet plum. He fishes in two worlds with the same rod and that rod is the pulse of inspiration. He walks the road during the full light of day yet none can follow on his footsteps. He seems not to breath or moan. There is no pain in him or his desires. Flowers and mountains guide him. He redeems himself in flashes of lightening, wisdom born in his soul.

For

many years men tried to conquer the objections between them. They composed armaments of metal to crawl and fly to destroy the civilizations they had designed and built. Unsatisfied with the words a certain neighbor spoke, even a neighbor in distant lands thousands of miles away unsettled them each. Was it wise for so many nations to operate a bank with so many fingers in it the weak and the strong complained? Many complain, so little is fair.

The

goals of war explode as shades of falling darkness from the sky in men's mind. Red blood and once proud bodies stuffed now with broken bones lie like trinkets sprinkled on the ground. Mothers and daughters weep over the loss of fathers and husbands and brothers. The men of war at it again carrying the flag of conflagration to historical battlegrounds against the common sense of objection. Foolishly tossing away the lives of men and women and children, strangers in their country, unable to say hello or goodbye. The language foreign and unusable. War gone beyond their borders. War on the ocean. War in the sky.

The
display of morning and evening locked in the cycles of the planets. Nine stones Mercury to Pluto spinning books revealing three epochs-past, present, and future. Beyond these thrones the heavens themselves provide a face of distant permanence. The objects of creation born to die.

Yet,
when a man is compared to the days of the heaven there is no sound at all. The war of man is not with his brother or sister or father or mother or their children, not his friends or his so-called enemies. Man is born with the limits of minutes. Much to do, little time to do it. The death of a man the death of consciousness. A step back into childhood, into fear and ignorance, into the animal world. The fire of anger opening a dark hole in the heart casting millions into a desert where there are no roads. The wise know they cannot travel without the eyes of the heavens to guide them.

Here,
says the eye of the prophet, see the land of wisdom, burrow in. Outside the region of the spinning planets fly with me to Epsilon or Arctarus or Sirius. These lights fire in the orb of Space. Where is the morning and evening, the guiding light, the symbols to make words, to create episodes that lead to war then peace among men? Out in Space mighty men are less than an army of worms.

Seso
offered the suffering to hold the lantern of golden flames in the minds great eye. Listen to the breath of the Cry of Beauty. The field of women and men planted here in soil growing spiritual limbs to heights unimaginable. They walk with the legs of giants. No more twisting tricks of blind men, mischief and deception, lies and fear tossed into the sea of peril.

Heed
the warning of the Book of Thorns. Living in the past will bring the repetition of decay and destruction. The law of creation goes forward, the roots of the plant goes down to hold its position, the stems and leaves struggle to receive a ray of light. Men must struggle to find the road to peace.

Each
sun spins on its on track. Each planet spins on its track around the sun. Each sun follows the wheeling galaxy. Each galaxy hums to its suns and the babies floating in its space. Each galaxy follows the arc of its covenant. Clearly these worlds, these suns, these galaxies rose into life from the same source.

Witness

the atom with its double suns, electrons on an endless, beginningless track. When was the day they began, they ceased spinning? The face of the atom not lost in Space. Spawned into creation from the skin of space. The original source the soil of creation, black Space; the lliving organism. The atom carries the words of history, what it has been and what it will be.

Seso

spins as the reward to open the eye of men, discharging his duties, removing the thorn lodged in the forehead of the lost. He wants all to know that men and women are positive and negative charges seeking the light of salvation. He wants all to know love is the crowning achievement. He wants all to know that the morning and evening we celebrate is limited only to the worlds flying in space around a sun. He wants all to know between the galaxies is not empty Space but the soil of life full of seeds yet to bear life.

LAST WORD

Look upon the galaxies in the heavens and count the number of stars in each. The comings and goings of my creation are so far beyond your reach it would be easier to balance a baby on a grain of sand. How can we explain to man his existence. The wise among you fatalistically cling to holy stakes driven in the ground thousands of years ago. Afraid to release themselves from their own false predictions of returning messengers. The boundary circumscribed by men walking in circles with books in their eyes and candles on the altars and bells clanging away the hours of time until all has been filled. How do we let them know that all will never be fulfilled because the journey did not begin here nor does it end here.

The
names of god continue to unfold newly formed. A babe for the soul of men to grow in to. The breath of each new messenger filled with the fire of the law washing out the old statues, stagnate and reeling from the generations of mankind trampling upon it until its word has no substance. Man subsists upon the vitality of a lliving word given by a lliving man or women. One whose spirit has been marked by time to walk the road with men and inspire them by their extraordinary style of living and wisdom. And when these entities come among you with the word of the day why do you look to the past for resurrection? Of what thing in all my creation have you seen that has been born again? I show you my days and nights and throw the wind across the sky and toss colors on all that is alive. There is no part of my creation that is not in motion and yet you put your eyes in the back of your head as if all my yesterdays were on a table that you could go to and look at a clear picture of all that has gone before. Did you think that when I raised my next messenger that he would call god Yahweh, Jehovah or Allah, Brahma or god almighty or the great I Am? Did you know in all your wisdom that my messenger would be Osiris or Buddha or Cyrus or Pythagoras or Zoroaster or Mohammed or Baha'u'llah?? Of the sixteen that came how many were symbols? You have accepted these men whether it be true or not because men have placed them in books and presented them as holy and not one of them existed before they existed. Yet, you count it strange that this one has come with a different mission than you knew. But you will not cease in your mental detective work and your spiritual wanderings because this one did not announce anything before making his presence known and HaHiYa seems so unlike a name you know. If this one would have spoken a word to save a man that had leapt from a burning building and landed on his feet or called out in a loud voice to stop the wars and those commandments obeyed then

you would have something to cheer about. You would have sought out his doorstep for counsel and miracles.

HAHIYA chose the path of this one. He is mine. I alone sit upon his heart and numbered its every beat and I alone spoke in his soul and visited him in his dreams. I made him a separate thing so that none could say that they had tampered with him or falsely claim that they had a hand in his doings, in his comings and goings. I give him the last word and the first and in every way showed this one my divine creation, its beauty and its wisdom. And those few who saw him that felt they knew him recognized that some spiritual adventure was occurring caught a glimpse of me shining through his eyes.

The

spirit of HaHiYa manifesting in the soul of Seso needs no measuring cup. It needs no stage to cast nets or magic potions. It is the lliving reality of holiness blessing all in its presence whether they know it or not. It is the rainbow of truth rising daily from the seed of the Cry of Beauty and it is a tree of bountifulness that spreads the winds of love. Put your hands in its waters and wash your faces and your backs and feel the rivers of peace flow into your bones. Close your eyes and

drift into its heavens, into its galaxies of the heavenly abode for the spirit of you is eternal. It has no beginning and no end.   You exist in the hand of HaHiYa always

FIDANCE-SEAL OF LEGAT

When

Jake Motto passed from this world he wrote in his final commentary The Seal of Legat the pathway of maintaining the structure of the Heb. The Koba's, the circle of sixteen divided into three units of five Koba's to be the guiding lights of the three aspects of The Heb: Ancestry, Signs and Symbols, and Becoming. The head of the Thorns of the Rose, So'Ya's security force, provides a box of sixteen flowers from which each Koba picks one. The Koba with the longest flower will become its head servant as was Seso and Jake Motta, after those gifts no longer lived in this world and I inherited the title as Za'Koba of The Cry of Beauty. And the Za'Koba shall remain in this office for a period of fifteen years. The first three years of Za'Koba is to visit the flowers in the spectrum of the community.

Only

in the presence of the people can the Za'Koba know what is in the land where the followers live. Only then can one know the needs of the people. The hill is an advantage only to survey the overall struggle but intrigue is not on the hill, intrigue is down below, in the lives of men and women and children and society and government. The Za'Koba has to be among the soljahs and the people to witness their daily triumphs and failures. How can men speak if they are not in the same place or if they know not the language and style and customs of the day? The Cry of Beauty is not an unchanging river; it flows through the heart and the mind and the soul. It is not alive yesterday only but seeks to answer the questions and challenges of today.

Let

it be known as I fix these words in this my Seal of Legat that I have tried in every way possible to fulfill the obligations of the Za'Koba and have submitted myself to The Cry of Beauty. So many seasons of change have come and gone. I admit I have known days of feeling overwhelmed and inadequate in the face of changes beyond the power of men. So many lost in the days of earth changes and wars. We join together as spiritual fishermen in the great sea of HaHiYa's ocean.

Seso

was once a voice alone. He knew homelessness and suffering of one who was pursued by a relentless enemy, the almanac of intrigue on full display. HaHiYa set Seso spinning and those of a loving nature were drawn within his circle and those of mischief were spun away. Seso multiplied and we became the lliving tree we call The Heb. The sacrifices he made opened the Ocmaba, the pathway of the Koba. Fixed like a star at night, an anchor in the wind unmoved by the onset of slaughter round about. The eye set in the center of the halfmoon counts the hours of peace without moving. We who have become Koba's unfold the wings of mysteries looking past the gate to the road Wonderful and surrender the body of life for life. We know we must go down to come up. Only in that moment of silence can the transition be made and then you know what you could not have known before that time has passed. For who could know what may come upon you to make a change of mind. Did you see the day when the valleys became hills and the hills became mountains and the lowlands disappeared? A new nest for birds and insects changing course to keep pace with the virgin sugar bush recently growing wild on hillsides. So many changes and the end of wars as many nations struggle to survive in the new world a vision of creation.

The

clock of HaHiYa fulfilling its own purpose. A strong current carrying away the willing and the unwilling. Are men pawns or have they chosen wisely escaping to the high country of spiritual insight? Those who were prepared scurried to the mountains as the earth heaved to and fro. Slowly returning to valleys of intrigue clinging to the book for relief.

HaHiYa

I have sung your praises many days. I came through the winter of life when it seemed all was lost or perished. I felt the breath of spring and began to see new things unfold. A new joy in the spring season of planting and tending the garden of HaHiYa's plumes and foliage. The feet of many men and women awakening in new abodes of hope and spiritual delight. As this summer season begins to grow I am already in my season of fall soon to know the last winter of life. Released from this world my journey will continue to unfold in the coming world of splendor and wisdom.

I

surrender my title of Za'Koba and carry with me always the work in the fields of HaHiYa's many flowers in many nations. HaHiYa's word is abundance and those of us that know without doubt the benevolence of The Book of Subtraction, the less I have of myself the more I am able to serve and give away.

A

brother in the army of soljahs, a Do'Bah of So'Ya in the service of HaHiYa for the sake of The Cry of Beauty

peace and peace and peace

Za'Koba Fidance

my Seal of Legat

RISE AND CELEBRATE

See

those lights, iridescent in broad bands undulating around the arctic cap, they are the visible clapping of the hands of magnetism. This northern rainbow requires the mind of men to wonder at the revelations creation bestows and unfolds. The fields of endless miles of snow as silent as the sky overhead reflected in the mirror of Lake Erie in a early morning moment. The moon and the stars sailing across the endlessness of the heavens against the blackness of space.

What

wondrous thought came to the mind of those witnesses that first realized the Sun hesitated in its journey South before turning from its long fall and began to rise through the ice of winter. This place we call home, in our little spot in creation was given signs and symbols so that we could partake in creation's wisdom. A sense of knowing, a feeling, the animal instinct to become aware of forces operating beyond what we could see or hear or touch. For the heavens are more than we with their seeming permanence. Never experiencing mortal beginnings and endings withholding their stories for the future. Only revealed after many thousands of generations. And even at this late date with all our advancement we still inch forward with a death grip on what men said was truth five thousand years ago.

The

armies of truth still die on old battlefields. Suns with undiscovered worlds await us. Each with stories and lights of many colors gathering at the North and South angles, a defined destination, of pause, the arc of the covenant, where heavenly praise murmurs, slowly rises, almost imperceptible and then gathers speed as the spring of bountifulness appears suddenly on the horizon.

When

those first witnesses came to this knowing they rose up and celebrated. They came with the news of a wonderful event. Those witnesses saw the signs in the heavens and so they marked their hearts and their souls. Rise and Celebrate. Tell all you know, that you see, a great truth has been revealed in the heavens and it comes yearly and after the moon has come with a full face three times the ice will fade and the earth will flower again. Rise and celebrate and give thanks. Heavens book has revealed for all men to see the pathway of giving begins in a fading light and a single star to announce everything is alright. A feeling of specialness clings to the air as the harvest of fall is consumed.

Once

a year hope for tomorrow appears. HaHiYa has given us this gift of reading his creation and so I share this gift with you.

Rise and Celebrate   Rise and Celebrate

It may be winter but spring is soon to appear. We know the true sign and it is the witness of a future bounty.

ZERO

The
apex of the circle slips backwards to mark time. There is no *Point* where nothing exists. The disc in space above us is a frequent site spinning, falling through absolute space. Men saw the first number and called it savior. Its light standing still and then rising and then rising again with a bride full of light pregnant with children sprouting to making their way on earth.

Who
is this maker of numbers? Is it the gases spun into suns into globs expelled as matter trekking on tireless wheels? Even the eye of man has never seen nothing. Man counts each form beginning always at one. How can man be a witness in creation without counting? Grabbing the many forms to extend each boundary is not a war of complacency.

When
the bird sings its melody or the thunder strikes it makes a vibration that waves its hand and creation listens. Each note a complete utterance of all that existed before. The waves of heat and cold, fast and slow, high and low, rhythmic patterns of nine chasing one another into more and more forms, unique in design and purpose with a place to call home. Each note with a beat.

This
is the story of numbers, the existence of life. There is no thief here that made nothing. There is an underskin bright with seeds rooted in the soil of space. The escaping gases whipping themselves into a feverish pitch, yelling in galactic fields to come together. Millions upon millions upon millions of years turning galactic fields into beds of baby suns. Each new beginning written in the journals imprinted on the atoms merging into molecules merged into hydrogen, neon, helium, nitrogen, oxygen, carbon and silicon and gold and iron, light that merged into globs emerging planets emerged into molten and metal and condensation into atmosphere, distilled as water and other vapors solidified as soil sprouting spores of living things and man, a being of selfconsciousness. All of this counting once begun multiplying itself over and over and establishing rules and conditions.

And
men pointed their finger giving the forms names. Nowhere did the eye of man fall upon Nothing because the witness of zero did not exist, nor has ever existed.

The
age of science came with the laws of manipulation, systems of division and separating life into pastures where living things could be contained. Stepping away from the musical scale and counting numbers into the trillions using a minus for all things too small that have a value less than the disc, which was always a one, a savior. What are all these things but what men have conceived in their minds. Agreeing among themselves they have reached the final truth.

Galaxies
cycling in space nothing more than so many millions of beans falling in a jar. Space not alive? but dead? with burping holes exploding into view on a known day when all its atoms were counted giving rise to the formulae of time, the distance between two forms unable to occupy the same space. More theories of time emerging. Scientist afraid if they go too far they will not only discover themselves on millions of planets but that they will reach the ending edge and fall off into an abyss of nothing or Space that can't be explained at all.

Say
to man that this creation is full of repetition and for proof look at the heavens. Are not the lights of the deep the same as the sun that gives man life? There is not one tree on earth but many, there are not one people but many people. There is not one raindrop but many raindrops.

Everything that is done in this Creation is repeated over and over. This creation has neither arrogance or ignorance, it is made with beauty and wisdom and without err whether man knows it or not. Nor is the creation made so that any one thing is permanent but all forms here come to their life and then pass on for there are other fields to see and experience what men call lliving. It is a song of beauty, sadness and joy, moments we share, us and the creation. It is only after men have travelled that they come to know what they did not know was truth. Speculate mankind on the immensity and then figure out the journey the same way that you go about seeking out each other's heart for existence. Surely man is a perpetual child sitting with bated breath wondering how all this came to be and still with all his tools the mystery remains as elusive as it did yesterday.

THE BOOK OF CLARITY

The children of the Sun trail after her on an endless track. Each child writes in its own book its clock of destiny. The most ancient of histories, tales, and legends presented on leaves speaks of man as a most ancient being. Above the head of mankind in a field of blackness is a swirling cloud of shiny dust spiraling on a road. The Milky Way one of countless numbers of galaxies spinning in lliving Space. The most ancient of legends alive in the mind of the most ancient of peoples.

Once the number of the children that flew around the Sun was thirteen. These children were of different types and meanings. These were the people that were most ancient journeying from beyond these realms for settlement. The conflagration that erupted over time caused the destruction of these worlds and the surviving people made their way to the third planet, smaller but heavier and denser. The people that came from one were large, their world large, older, and less dense. The other people came from a world a little smaller, warmer, and heavier but larger than earth. They were of the same family, one more ancient than the other. These people of different hues of brown made an agreement not to war. Over time what knowledge they had they lost. Many of these travelers did not know the science of the worlds they had come from and the strange creatures that roamed the ground on this new world and the diseases of this world took the lives of many. After many generations what were once wise people slipped into a nocturnal sleep of fables and wonders of flying machines and giant buildings. The few things that remained were the traditions and simple rules of order. The man would lead and the woman and the children would follow. The earth itself roiled separating the people and they became tribes and then nations separated by land and language. Few words were common so men could no longer speak directly to one another. It was this fear that brought war again among the people who no longer knew that they were the descendants of two people that had intermingled their blood and their ways. Five times men subdued the earth only to fall again into chaos and darkness. Leaving behind the stone edifices and written documents of their rise to power and order. The discovered ancient history by the newest power was hidden away fearing what the people would do if they knew truth. Secret groups were created to keep this '*wisdom*' from the common man. The leaders made themselves the Sun of the people and placed themselves on thrones on earth. They said to the people, bend your knee before your king for I alone am the light, the same as the Sun in the heavens for it is from the heavens that I am descended and it is there I will return. Then men made different people, those who would lead and those would follow. Those who would lead became the mind for all the people and made all decisions. Those who would follow would do all the labor and make all the discoveries. All that they would sow would be a benefit to the leaders and when it came time to reap they would only get a ten percent share.

The days when these people exist has passed in the heavens. This ancient idea wobbles now on its last leg. It is the vesture of Armageddon and has been summoned to be cast into the fires of the past. The book speaks of the new way not the old. The book speaks of the new people not the old. The book speaks of the new traditions and rules not of the old. As the old woman pours water from her pitcher as she has done before she sings, the new way will fly man into a new world and once again his heart will open, his mind will fill with light, and his spirit will sit in the silence of peace.

So we speak to the parent of the child. Although you may be of a different height one is not more or less than the other. Though your body's have different instruments the music you can make is still music. One cannot be the other nor can one be denied because the soul comes a moment too early choosing another path for the body. When the sands of the world have given men freedom then how can the leaders say men are no longer free? How then will leaders be able to strip the flesh of humanity and tell men they have privileges only or are obligated to this nation or this religion when they know full well all these things are false creations of men who have hidden and denied the existence of ancient texts and lost histories. Will they continue to meet in secret to control the destiny of all mankind when they are so few?

So we speak of the parents of the children.

When men came to this world and had fallen it was trial and error that led them. What to eat and what to drink. Observing animals like themselves they touched plants and fruits and leaves. The Sun and Moon gave them the cycles of life. Natures book of silent words, symbols that man gave a name and a place. They took unto themselves the patterns around them of the wolf, spiders, bees, ants, burnt out hulls of trees floating on rivers, vines and blossoms organized into families and kept as a sistory (stories of learning). They made the Sun a lliving character acting in their daily lives that all things submitted to and praised. They made the Moon the guide of the night to help travel through the darkness. It was the Sun and Moon they made that kept life together. So, the nation made them the pattern for the government. All lesser things would be in orbit of those who sat on the high throne and were made to be sacred, as only those in that position could use that power, the same as the Sun over its subjects in the heavens. Now man could begin his ascension anew without falling into chaos and darkness. Man could now rise as the most ancient of legends said he had been before. Man could go into the heavens and be among the gods. So they understood they needed tools to subdue the earth and all its inhabitants. Ideas too close to the truth were cast aside. Men who sought change led mankind into war. Soon smaller Suns and Moons rose to take power. War and the power of men subdued the woman. All mans wisdom was now carried in the hand of a man. As mans wisdom gained speed the emotion to control ran over the edge like a waterfall. Men ruled men turning the earth into fields of blood and lies. The wisdom of the ancients kept even further from the masses and many of the leaders of the men. One here and one there kept this now truly secret and sacred knowledge of where man came from and where one day he would return. They knew it would take many years so this idea was made into a secret for only a few and was told to the masses as the day when heaven would be on earth again and written in books as the day when a great soul (the resurrection of the hidden truth) would return.

The
laws of creation are simple enough. The plant is nourishment, animals eat one another, air is a chemical process as is water acted upon by the Sun and Moon without which no living thing could exist here. Has not man copied these laws? Man is a tiller, a tinkerer, and a manipulator always expanding his part of the earth. All of mans work is supposed to be for goodness. All of mans rules and traditions are supposed to be for goodness. Let the parent ask when did the path change and men began to hurt the children, the generations of his seeds?

So
we speak to the parent of the children. Who is the child, the parent or the child? What does the child know unless the child is given the food from the parent? The parent is a form of wisdom and patience. The child is a listener and an unbridled adventurer. The rules of eating and walking are the first the child learns. The rules of speaking and society come early. Then come the rules of traditions. The rules of tradition contain the rules of limitation and celebration. The child carries these rules for life once formed. The child according to its nature then will either rebel or come to terms of acceptance of many of these rules. The Family of the Rulers of mankind will always seek to ensure that no great change occurs because the family of man has been taught to be obedient. No one wants to go out into the ocean and stir a tempest for fear of drowning.

So
we speak to the parent of the children. The first lesson of the speaking child are the sistory of family. This is Ancestry. The second lesson of the speaking child are counting and understanding

the naming of things. This is Signs and Symbols. The third lesson of the speaking child are the questions of the life. This is Becoming. The children each have their own path to walk. If the parent is a music maker and a baker, a husband and a wife, is the son to be a music maker or the daughter a baker? Because we wear the same shoe does not mean we are the same. The gift of the child will show itself as the days pass. If there is no war then the child can find its way. If there is war or war has ended then the nation is lost and all must find their way as best they can. Some of the children are born with the talent already in their hands and the road for them has less fog. Others have no visible talent, its lies deep within their minds, stunted by the shocks of too much aggression around them. These are the seeds that lay on the soil that need more nourishment and nurturing if the time permits. Warfare is the great plague of man, throwing life into chaos and darkness producing those giants leading mankind into a cave from which they might not retrieve themselves for many generations. The parent must always watch for the child whose head is fearful and bigger than everyone else's. This is the child that cares not for the lessons of Ancestry, Signs and Symbols, and Becoming because they are all the laws unto themselves and are dark pioneers and pilots riding the rocky seas. They cannot see the land because all the past is there and the boat they want to Captain is out in the sea.

So

the parent of the children is to give these lessons and more. Is not the parent to show the man and woman love? The unit of oneness the cornerstone of peace. A child is the only addition a family should know. If the family suffers subtraction that is a discharge that takes from everyone. The cornerstone is broken and even if replaced it is not the original. The house and all its rooms will feel the difference. The feeling of union once disrupted will continue to ripple into the next generation as a sistory. Parent be mindful of your choices; your seeds are watching to see if you make only flowers and vines they can wrap themselves them around and grow. If you produce weeds they will infiltrate the garden of the children. No one knows how a weed will infect a child not alive long enough to know the history of weeds and how to live wisely with them. The parent knows having seen the effects of weeds and smile in themselves because they know. Weeds and words and wolves and floods and fire and illness, living and dying, are the stages men know after having lived long enough to witness them at work. Survival becomes the goal. How can the parent teach the children to survive and not succumb to these aspects of living if they themselves are sliding in snow?

So

we speak to the parent of the children. The children have reached the age of responsibility. Soon they will be out of your sight and join the nation. Pray that the nation is not at war and the children become lost in a foreign country or become infected with the fear of taking life or giving life on a battlefield far from home. If the nation is quiet and doing its business send the child away with what gifts you can give them. The bird cannot leave the nest if it can't fly but if it stays in the nest it will die. The children come through the parent only to one day create space for themselves. If the child has found itself in Ancestry, Signs and Symbols, or Becoming then the initial contract, they will have with life has begun. Each child is responsible for the food that goes in their mouth and the clothes to cover themselves. If the child desires more than the parent then the child must understand what it means to be a tall tree not just another branch. There are many small Suns each shining with its own light attracting to it its own Moon and all the other things that make heaven a wonder to look upon. The child must understand only so much can be done alone that is why all that lives in creation lives because other things are alive here too.

So

we speak to the parent of the children. Now that death is near and all the children are older what has been taught to the children of dignity and how to divide the spoils of life. Has the parent been wise and written down how to provide for the last days? How do the children know how to proceed the days after the death of the parent?

These are the rules:

The

parent is to write down the gifts to be given to the children whether it is gold or silver or paper, the child or children are to provide meals for the visiting family and friends, the children are to present themselves as they were raised, the celebration after four days is for the remembrance of the parent, the witnesses of friends are to speak on the life of the parent for they knew them best, body is to be disposed of by fire or casket according to the wishes of the parent, the children of the parent are forbidden to violate or plunder the home of the parent nor are they to take up residence if they did not live there, the parent is to make certain the family knows special agreements for the children, anyone who violates the rules of dying cannot participate in the transfer of any gifts or for the rest of their life be recognized as one would see a fox or any other animal of plunder without regard for innocence of a circumstance. Those family members identified as criminals will not be denied a reduced inheritance; no punishment will be advanced against the children of a criminal unless they too become a criminal. The family must come to the aide of the criminal's children; showing them love and assisting them in walking the right path of understanding. The children of the mother with no father must be looked upon as all children of the family and receive no slights, nor should the mother be struck with meanness and ill will. The man who father's children is always the father of those children because they carry his seeds. The father of unwed children is to provide for those children and look after them and not transfer this responsibility to any other man. Neither a man or a woman is a spout, have no more than two if they are not under your roof. The man and woman of unwed children are equally responsible for the raising and care of their child. If the man or woman is found to be sabotaging the rearing of their child then that parent is to be taken into court. If there is fighting then both parents must submit to counseling for mental balancing. These are the reasons that from the beginning each parent is to be wise; what is the difference in rearing each other and rearing a child? Is not the parent a child coming together to make a union? To learn love and not cast each other aside or display undue anger or chastisement or resentment for these things are a transfer residing in the heart and mind of the child that must one day exhibit themselves.

So
we speak to the parents of the nation.

The
nation has raised itself by the work of its children. The people have invented rules and traditions to walk daily under an umbrella of their own making. This is the law that a few men had a hand in making. These were the men thought to know what was best for the people and make a nation upon a land that they said belonged to all. Once the next day came the nation became two people, the leaders and workers.

So
we speak to the parent of the nation. The nation is the people. It is the house of the people. It is the road of the people. If the leader of the nation is ill then it is up to the people to help him get well or remove him. The leader of the nation is not a single man or woman that can go off and make deals in secret and give his friends gifts or toss visitors into the sea. The leader of the nation says he feels insulted because a leader of another nation won't let him take what he wants just because he is more powerful with his army of warriors. The warriors of the nation are not his alone to order to attack or retreat because he is pretending to act like the Sun. The Sun sails in the heavens of his realm and never changes, all in his realm follow his lead. When did the leader change? When did the new leader change the old rules if they were working? Why does he now say the engine is not working? Who broke or added a part that made it make noise as if it were broken when it was just the smoke of too much oil. The small Suns and Moons have changed faces and hand off to others their duties because they have all become drunk with power. So the parent of

the children sits at the table with food on their plate from a foreign country because the nations crops failed. All the forks and knives cheap imitations the nation no longer makes. The parent admits to himself he was silent too long while the nation prepared to take up arms. I don't want to go to war, the parent is heard saying to his wife. The parent of the children, all of them must never be silent. Death awaits his neighbor if he is quiet. His neighbor is the man in his country and the man in the country of his enemy. The parents of the nations have voices and must not let the leaders spoil the lands with blood and finger pointing, the way to discrimination and anger a shroud over their eyes as they seek destruction.

If

there is peace in the land then the house can make its own shoes and clothes, take their own machines to make tools and all that the nation needs. When the nation does not make at least two thirds of what it needs with its own machines then the nation is in peril. The parent of the child cannot go borrowing nor can the nation. The orders of the nation are the same as the parent:

The

parent of the child needs to work, if there are no machines they cannot work, if there are no machines other parents in other nations will use their machines to make what the nation needs. If there is not enough food it has be brought to the nation. If there is hunger in the nation then anger becomes the parent. If there is anger then there is fear. If there is fear then there is crime. Crime leads to oppression; oppression leads to rebellion. The behavior of the parent is falls. The parent looks away from the children; away from the home; looks into the eye of disappointment. The child looks away from the parent. The fields of separation once sowed are hard to mend. The smaller suns and moons begin to chew on the heels of the nation. They become importers of darkness leading others into darkness. Other nations feed on this blood in the water; the discord flares countless times spreading the issue the ways of peace are lost for a time. The navies of nations take to the sea. Men speak with overly sharp tongues at everything that moves because nothing is right.

The

proper tool one day comes to the mouth of one that has had enough leading men once again to a balance of what is right and wrong and how things should be done. If they speak to one another from one nation to the next and not seek to get an angle then men can once again listen.

The

parents of the children must know as does the nation that laws are not for the citizen, the parent, laws are for the criminal. What law does the parent need when his house is one of discipline,

organization, and smiles. Does not the parent of the children know the difference between right and wrong? Are not his steps counted by the behavior of his children? Are not his eyes focused on the path of his children and the direction in which they are walking and talking? Who has the parent fought with yesterday or the day before? Who has he angered today? Tomorrow the parent takes his son to the barbershop and the mother takes her daughter shopping. The car goes to the mechanic. The dress has to be mended. The parent talks to the teachers and takes the children to the doctor. The parent and their friends go to ball games and fishing. The parent sits outside at night while the children play and catch lightening bugs or
chase butterflies in the park not far from the lake. The parent listens to the children read stories and work out numbers from Signs and Symbols. The parent does not lie in wait to steal any person or their possessions. The parent does not sit up at night scheming ways to be tricky or spread false rumors to bring a neighbor down. No one is looking for the parent or his children so what does the parent need a law for. To tell the parent how to behave? The parent is following the example already laid out in the pattern of the cornerstone, the foundation of the house which has not changed in thousands of years.

Only
if a parent pretends not to know what goodness is does he need to be bound by a law and that in itself is a crime for which only Time is the remedy. Only the light of wisdom can make these things pass away. Only love can penetrate past anger and fear. You parents, that walk in this darkness have missed the light of the Sun and turned your head from the Moon shining in the night sky.

So
we speak to the parents of the children.

The
Bond was always the simplest consideration that all men used to exchange goods and services. The parents feed and house each other, man and woman and the children as a unit. The sweetness of the woman a fire for the labors of the man. They made a Bond; love and fairness of the heart, labor, and the exchange of commitment.

So
the parents became millions in number. They made villages and cities and nations. They made roads and converted the land into patterns of agriculture. They grew and divided the labors making commerce. Acting out the roles of nature building and sowing and reapers of water and land. No longer bound to the hunt and wandering. This was the second Bond for all the surplus, trade among all peoples. It was in the Marketplace where the parents of the children met. They

made celebrations and holidays and days of labor and days of rest following the patterns of the Sun and the Moon. Man made Time to work for all occasions.

So
the parents of the children made rules. They meet and speak about the Bond. They meet with their eyes and they will speak words. The consideration of labor and scales used as proof of the value of produce to measure all exchange never less or more than five percent and apply the factor of distance and quantity delivered to the Marketplace. And so the value of the earth became the standard of exchange and its value the number of the population tenfold. No matter how full the well it can never overflow or recess causing economic distress. a value inexhaustible, constant.

The
aura of glamour is in this arena. The settlements of men from the houses of surplus. Even lands across the sea participants in the Bond, a known measurement. Are not the fruits of Nature's families lliving proof how man can protect the Bond from exhaustion and bloating? The cycles of Creation are in the billions of years of Becoming and continue unabated in the infinity. The supplies of Creation seeds in Space. The trees of earth, the waters, the plants and animals recycled annually. Even the soil added to by the death of earths living things. The inbreathe and out breathe of the pulsating Sun and winds sweeping across the mountains and low lands.

If
man is to sustain his supplies then the fields of commerce have to be level. The work of nature alive in fields of abundance growing out of decay. A single tree multiplying itself by branches and fruits. Falling fruit and nuts filed with seeds spread by the wind. The work of the family of insects and worms complete the cycle. When men multiply the surplus of goods but if they increase the value of exchange without regard to the value they impose an imbalance. The addition of an annual increase lessens some workers and adds more value to others. Nature is constant man is not. The glamour of some houses rains on others scattering the Marketplace, changing the Bond to favor a few. Here on this table we see men occupy time as a reason to change values and give it the name progress. The few manipulating the supplies of earth claiming that the new cycles cause an increase in the value of things. Removing the idea of the Bond as a constant labor and value known to all at the Marketplace. Highlighting in the modern world of technology by advertisements cheering the idea of hard work for equal rewards, creating levels of society viewed as the classes of men. How long before the loss of the constant Bond leads to ruin and rebellion and all-out war? Why does the marketplace require change? It is not a thing of time? The labor of one year is the same as the previous. And when men make inventions to decrease the labor the

yield from the field increases. How then is it that the wealth finds itself deposited in the hands of a few? It is not a mystery but trickery. The parents of children, who are the many must set a limit on the massing of commerce so that the surplus does not fall into the hands of a few. The idea of increases of the yield exchanged at the Marketplace must be a constant measurement not to rise or fall more than a one half percent in any five year period. Some men are wiser than others and will by their nature realize a net savings more than others but not so that their gathering is so large the scale of society tips overwhelmingly in their favor. Life must reflect the constancy of Nature so that the supplies of the earth are never misused or overused because of the greed and power of a few.

So

the parents of the children apply the lessons of the Bond to the material world that man has created. It is man who removed the trees and bushes and flowers to make roads. It is man who blocks waterways and makes lakes and takes down forests. It is man who makes roads in the sky and flies like birds. It is man who makes laws and rules of limitation. It is man who makes all things that nature does not. None of what man makes has a life of its own. None of what man makes has a seed that will grow wild in the fields or grow to a height and weight and color on its own. Mans inventions are Science Fiction. They come from mans imagination spawned by the revelations alive in Creation that man copies. It is the living language that men learn that inspires man to copy what he sees. It is the reason man cannot aspire to be a criminal, committing violations in a Creation whose origin is divine. It is one thing to know to not know an effect of the technology it is another to create fictitious limits and say that it was inspired by a god. The Bond of Peace is sufficient. What is the purpose of a book of thousands of pages with law upon law to confuse the many? It is the criminal that needs to be judged and that judgment is simple enough. Those that

take what is not theirs and have reached an age of maturity will be bound and questioned and punished according to an agreement of the ages. Those who work outside of the Bond will lose an amount equal to the theft and labor to match the amount of loss until it is equaled and given to the injured party. Injury to others unless it is for protection of self or an act of war will not go unpunished. Men will not be allowed to repeatedly injure others. If it is a person between the age of twelve and fifteen the parent will be responsible for payment of loss and the child and parent will be extra supervised and counseled until the age of eighteen. If the child commits a violent act resulting in sever injury to another then the child will be taken to a home for counseling and the parent must attend weekly lessons. Any person who knowingly takes the life of an innocent person then that criminal will be removed from society for counseling and education and nourishing for a period not to exceed twenty five years. Those who manipulate the Marketplace for false gain will find themselves working as labors in the Marketplace for a period of two years without compensation except room and food. Those individuals will receive weekly counseling concerning the meaning of the Bond and its use for the benefit of all and not for trickery by a few. The family of the accused must also be active participants. No person should ever feel that they are alone in the world and that all have rejected and abandoned them. The family of the criminal will not be lessened by others either in treatment or invitation. Not everyone who comes to this life is at peace with themselves or others and it is not the fault of the parent if the child goes astray unless the parent themselves are mutations and full of evil intent. If it discovered that the parent is abusive then it is the parent who will suffer loss along with the child.

The same word that supplants the family speaks to the nation. The nation is the great tree with boughs and branches. The purpose of the nation is to be a shelter for the people. It the house of protection and the hand that is extended to all other nations. It is the doorway to exchange across the seas. Its skin the border and the face the government known by all men at home and abroad. Those who present themselves to act as leaders are servants of the Bond directing the constant theme to ensure that the nation neither falls into disarray or conducts itself in a way that leads to war or criminal activity. When the nation has balance it cannot fall or make the mistakes of the old world nations full of enmity, greed, useless laws, finger pointing, division of the people because of religion, race, orientation, status, standing armies of civil or military; and destruction of the land, water, and air.

Let men know that life is best when it has a constant theme not rooted in false cycles of increase but in the natural growth of expansion where change comes because men have outgrown the past they have created. The fields of Space are calling men to come out as did the lands across the seas. Man is to be an adventurer in Creation. If men are not free how can they travel to new worlds? The words of the ancient texts will no longer suffice for those things which are to come.

A WORKER IN THE FIELD

Man

is a flowering seed hopping across the face of Creation. Written on the walls of creation are the mechanics of machines to help men to fly. The road leading up to the mountains of revelation where the spirit operates the mind. The body of man as old as the suns. Did not man come alive in the same gas fields spinning suns into existence? They are surely beings of light with their own purpose filled with the same elements. The atom speaks of this magic binding substance with memories of fingerprints on all that walks through the galaxies. Let this potion take a hundred million years of swirling gas crescendo to a spark igniting the lights filling the countless galaxies whirling gracefully in the deep.

Man

comes to this existence housed in flesh. He is a worker in the many fields growing here. Bearing seeds from the fields he has worked before. He comes as male and female energy. He comes as a conqueror, a destroyer and the beggar to be fed. The human comes as the beautiful woman all adore, some full of mischief and remorse. He comes as the hero and the clown. He comes as the artist of vision. The being of reason, pusher of dreams, the questioner and the expander of boundaries.

A

child comes forward as if by magic down a tunnel of darkness and says, mother do you remember when you woke up in this world?

The

grandmother knowing her life is slipping away looks at the words of the child with wonder.

Come here child for soon my days will end.

You remember when you woke up in this world grandma?

My memory is split from childhood to being grown so I run back and forth. One day I was just here.

Grandma that's what happened to me. I was playing with a ball outside.

So you knew it was a ball and you were outside?

Yes, grandma, it was me and my brother.

How do you think you knew that?

I don't know but I knew everything. The sky, the plants, the cars, my momma and daddy. I knew everything.

Yes, I bet you did. It won't be long and I'll be waking up in another place.

I know that, you mean when people die and leave here.

Yes, kind of like that.

Will you still be yourself or just a kid?

I don't know but I guess either way I'd have a lot to learn. It would be a new place to me. I'd have to learn to speak whatever language they use and I would have to learn how to move around. I would meet all kinds of people and figure out what I'm supposed to do.

You don't know what you're supposed to do? I know what I'm supposed to do.

What's that?

Play piano and build houses. Ever since I was little I knew that. Doesn't everybody know what they supposed to do?

Some do but there are a whole lot of people that don't. Some folks don't find out until they are old. Some folks never find out.

How come I know grandma?

I don't know child just another one of the mysteries of life.

Grandma I had no idea that time travels as quickly as it does.

Yes, it does go quickly. How old are you now?

I'm twenty eight now grandma.

Seems like just a couple of days ago you and I were sitting here at this same table, you couldn't have been no more than six or seven. You were asking me all kinds of questions about life.

I don't remember that at all. Do you miss my mother? She died so suddenly.

Yes, I do every day. But I always knew she wasn't a strong person. Mother's know their children.

You were always strong weren't you grandma?

I didn't have much of a choice. After your grandfather left I had to hold the family together. Your momma and my other three.

Do you ever hear from Uncle Cross?

He writes a letter every now and then but then your Uncle Cross never was one for family. He was so angry when he found out your grandfather wasn't his father he never got over it. I made a mistake.

What happened grandma, what made you get involved like that.

Not much to say, I met him and it was like something just took over. You can't tell your heart who you gone like or dislike if it sees what has been missing. It was a bad thing though, really tore the family apart.

What ever happened to him?

He just left one day. Said it wasn't right. And that was that.

I remember one time you tried to tell me about this man you saw down at the lake. Some kind of teacher or something.

Oh yeah, that was Mr. Seso. Had the prettiest woman, Octavia was her name. He was the one that started that city Caseload after the earthquake. That's where a lot of people went too.

Yeah, he was something special. Went all over the country talking about a new way of seeking peace. Started this thing called the Ocmaba, based on his book The Cry of Beauty. I went to some of his meetings, even went to his place of teaching called the Heb. He did a lot for the people. Woke up the sleeping. I know it helped me to come out of that dark place I created for myself.

What was he talking about that made him so special?

Just a different way of looking at life. Had his own thoughts about life.

So was he really a prophet?

I don't think he was a prophet in the way that people think of prophets of old but he was a messenger. He called god HaHiYa-the hand of life. And he said the only rent HaHiYa ever asked of any man or woman was love. He didn't do no baptizing or collect tithes. If you joined the Heb you became a worker in the field, one of the flowers of creation. He told a story that I never forgot.

What kind of story? Can I read it?

No, this one was never written down that I know of unless one of his followers did. This was right after your mother died and all that stuff about me and my troubles came to light. That was one of the reasons I was down at the lake. I was feeling bad, my heart and my head hurt. I didn't even realize he was near me until he started talking. There was just a small group of them sitting around. It was about six thirty in the morning. His words took hold of me and I let him in. He walked right into my heart and head and told this story about a war of conscience between a man and a boy that lived around the corner from one another. The man name was Ulis and the boy's name was Krong. There was this girl that lived next door to Ulis, her name was Haidu. Ulis retired early from the military. He and his wife lived quietly. Ulis had a big back yard where he had a fine garden. At first Krong was a nice kid but as he got older the neighborhood changed and Krong changed with it. He ran around with a gang of bad boys but mostly stayed on the corners where the business were. For some reason he took it in his head that Haidu belonged to him and so he began to threaten any of the boys that wanted to talk to her. One day as fate would have it he took a hold of her arm and tried to force her to come with him in front of Ulis's house. She managed to pull away and ran up on Ulis porch. Ulis heard the commotion and came out. Krong stepped up on the porch.

Krong what's going on here? He took one look at Haidu's face and saw the fear in her eyes.

None of your business old man. Krong took a step toward Haidu with his hand extended as if to grab her.

Ulis stepped in front of Krong. Krong looked back at the street where several members of his gang were watching.

Krong you will be making the biggest mistake of your life if you move an inch toward this girl.

What are you going to do old man, stop me?

Krong you are on my porch. You think you run this neighborhood, running around scaring people with this little gang of thieves. You're a coward Krong. You hear me, a scared little boy and you're scaring this girl. You don't scare anybody standing on this porch, you understand.

No

one had challenged Krong in a long time, not since he got his reputation.

What the hell you doing Mr. Ulis, you've known me since I was a kid? I just want to talk to her, tell him Haidu. You don't want trouble with me now do you?

Get off my porch, get off my property and take those boys with you before you get yourself in too deep.

What you got a gun on you old man? You talking awfully tough.

I got something stronger than a gun, I got guts, something you don't have.

The

boys on the street couldn't hear the words of Ulis. They couldn't see the steel in his eyes and they couldn't feel what Krong felt. They couldn't feel truth when a man of intent speaks it but Krong felt I. He had the sense of an animal that knew when he was outmatched and it had nothing to do with the number of boys in the street watching. Krong tried to hold his head up as he backed off the porch and left a trail of steaming fear that entered his loins. He said not a word as he led his little band off the street and back to the corner.

Thank you Mr. Ulis. I'm sorry I got you involved in this. Krong is a real hot head. I'm afraid he might try to do something to you. I'm sure he's feeling quite embarrassed.

Don't worry about Krong, he'll be alright. He just needs time to grow up and remember what he was like when he was just a kid running errands and playing. He's not really as mean as he acts.

I hope you're right.

I hope so too. I'd hate to see him get himself hurt.

You would hurt him?

I'm not talking about me, I'm talking about life pinching him with one of its thorns.

A

few months after that, right before Halloween Krong got arrested for robbery. After the run in with Ulis he had gotten really bad. He had three fights and even pulled a gun on a stranger. The word on the street was someday his getting that old man for dipping.

I'm going to get that old bastard. One day. One day. I got to wait can't do it now but soon, maybe in the spring when he's out there in that garden planting and shit. Bury him out there with those beets he grows.

What did he say to you Krong? You walked off that porch like you wanted to kill something but you never said a word.

Nothing, but one of these days, you mark my words, every day has its dog and I am a dog.

Grandma now that I'm thirty five can you finish the story you started years ago?

What story?

The story of Krong and Haidu.

Didn't I finish telling you that?

No, grandma don't you remember you went to sleep that day and then I left the country to go to war.

You went off to war?

Yes, grandmother but I always wanted to find out what happened to that boy Krong.

Well, he proved to be something else according to that Mr. Seso fellow. So, I told you about what happened to him when he went to jail that changed everything?

No, I didn't know he went to jail. I think you were getting ready to tell me about his friend Coates and what happened to them.

Well, let me see if I can get it all straight in my head. It was such a long time ago you know.

That's ok grandma, take your time.

Here son take my hand and close your eyes. I'm going to take you back to the day when I first heard this story. You can see Mr. Seso himself, hear him tell the story of Krong and Haidu.

You can do that?

Ssshhhh, hold my hand, close your eyes, relax, come on he's starting to talk....

Seso

sat with his back to Lake Erie, the water coming ashore slowly in small waves. Octavia, Jake Motto, Fidance, Samala, two small boys and their grandfather sat around him on stones in a circle.

Seso spoke:

Once,

in the oldest of days men were bred like animals. This was after the time when women birthed men alone. The fields were then fertile and newly made and the divisions among men became commonplace all over the world. Then came the long silence when mankind lost its way. Some were sent to raise men; their efforts snuffed out by the discord and lies of a so-called modern machine. Its medicine false and full of toxins. The earth herself went into a field vibrating on the strings of one that was to come. Go and see to the soil, why it is whispering under the moon nothing will grow while this cloud of uncertainty hangs around the door.

Krong's

journey unfolded on a broken road. His steps divided into branches with leaves of many colors and varieties of different seasons. His father was a vine wracked with noise, bent by the whispers of men sending waves to deceive him. This believe could not pass to Krong. Krong came with his own bottles to drink from and it would be years until he knew from which to take a full swig.

Where

was the childhood of Krong? Without sweet things and toys to play with? Where was the brilliant light of love. A softer voice in his ear instead of the concrete and steers gathering with vacant eyes. Chewing on cud layered with disappointment. Krong grew on a back road with other children where there was someone to listen. It was on this road he met Coates. Krong took him to the streets, Coates took him shopping through back doors and roofs. Growing into young men tired of the tragedy playing raggedy music at home. Angry hands and scenes of screams, dry mothers, drinking and drugs infesting neighborhood nests.

Everybody

knew Ulis the farmer. Krong worked in his fields to escape home.

Krong it is time to stop, the wind is coming today. They would walk to the front of the garden and stand there.

Close your eyes Krong wait for the wind. Listen you can hear it passing the leaves. A lliving thing. Krong felt the wind pass him drifting over the garden. It was the first time he ever felt peace and then it was gone.

Time

is the great mover of mankind. Krong and Coates continued nicking themselves. Dark soldiers with cuts up their sleeves mouths open reporting to all who listened danger was the only tree they climbed. They extended branches of themselves to men like themselves making bargains and gaining entrance into the world under their feet.

Krong

always kept his eye in search of a way to snare Haidu. To him she was a rabbit, a mare he was unable to tame. More than once in her company the arrow of her rejection always hit the same place. Just above his heart, just below his throat and the words he thought so clever delivered out of place.

One

day she saw him being dragged away. A witness to Krong trying to stop a man from killing the wrong man shooting the man himself. It was the worst day of both their lives. The eye recorded it and the mind could not erase it. Haidu found herself on the porch of Ulis.

I never seen anything like that. I don't know why I feel so sad for Krong. Of all the things he should have been locked up for this is not the one.

Krong was a good kid growing in a place that needs to eat and the food is boys like him.

There ought to be something we can do. Look at this neighborhood. Look at all the neighborhoods where we live. Grown men walking around like its recess. I never thought it would be like this. I thought that by the time we got grown a lot of those boys would have stopped acting like little gangsters. Now they out here just killing each other.

It takes time to make a man. The way things are now with no hope for a future because there aint no work it takes even longer for these boys to become men if they make it.

Poor Krong.

Do you love him Haidu.

No, but I've known him all my life and its just sad how he turned out.

Well, he's still alive maybe in time he'll grow up, if not he'll just be one more brother laboring under the ground.

Laboring under the ground?

Restless soul, disappointment.

Krong got ten years for attempted murder. The government made money on the dead alive in a jail cell. Coates joined him two years later on a burglary charge. The rounds of this infernal rang the bell the beginning of each year. The steel tomb was so unforgiving, not caring about any man, not fearing what could become of skin showing cuts. Krong and Coates learned the techniques of survival and slowly began to thrive arriving at a place of respect as two hardened men. What then makes a man do the unexpectant, go against established rules, stick his nose in a noose salted with pepper. Jail is no place for a holy man mistaken for a sweet meat. The new prize was thought to be a sheep and was to be stripped and toppled to get at his tender meat. Krong came upon the event and could not walk away.

Krong you know we cannot mix in this. He has been chosen by Isech. We can't get involved with Isech. It would be like turning in your mother to the police.

Have you heard him? Did you hear that man talking the other night? That stuff about the Cry of Beauty and The Day of Subtraction? Did you hear those words, what they meant?

I heard it Krong but who is he? Who is this Seso fellow? A prophet? Com'n man you know I'll do anything with you, you know how we roll but this, no. You do this on your own. What you got three years left? You think you can survive here three years if you step into Isech's alley? No way, nobody could.

They
tell me Krong took one last look at his friend Coates and said: Sorry but I can't let it go down like this.

Then you gonna die Krong, you gonna die man.

Then I die.

Krong saved my worker that day. His name was Balcon. Balcon had not fully recovered from his old life and had begun hanging out with his old crowd at the bar. One night someone got killed and he was charged as a codefendant. During the fifteen months he sat in county jail he reclaimed his life and began the process of awakening his soul. By the time he finally got to prison eighteen months later he was a more rarified human. The inmates saw a gentle clean soul upon which they could feast. Krong stood before them a wall they could not penetrate. The battle that ensued was a testament to the strength within him and at least ten fell before he was taken down. The men feasted on Balcon and he died taking his own life. Krong who had stood so broad among his peers was fastened with a title Small Bridge in reference to the stand he had made and failed. He and Coates would not see things the same again for many years.

I
got a letter from Krong the year after Balcon died. I sent him the information he requested. I never heard from him again. But I did hear about the things he did once he got home. Haidu sent me a letter telling the last part of his story:

Dear Seso

first, I want to thank you because I know it was because of you that Krong finally became the man I did not know was in him and became the man I love and married. I should say loved because he has passed on but he is so alive in my heart it is as if he has not died at all. I want to tell you about his life after prison and the wonderful things he did.

He

came to my house so changed I didn't recognize him at first. He was nearly forty years old. He spent fifteen years in prison because of all the fights he fought just to stay alive. The last three years he survived because he was transferred to another prison. His friend Coates had been home twice and back in jail, a career criminal. I did not know about the drama between them. I could see by the look in his eyes that the old Krong I remembered was gone and standing before me was just a man hoping to start a new life. It wasn't pity or anything like that I felt for him it was in the beginning me giving respect to a fellow human being and someone I had known all my life. It was the words he said that took hold of me and the sound of sincerity in his voice.

Am I home?

What?

Am I home, Wilema? And he just stood there looking so deep in my eyes I felt myself floating.

Wilema? You know that's not my name.

One who wades in river water, Wilema. That's what they told me. They cleaned me up Wilema in river water that came from the soul and so I stand here before you and ask you am I home Wilema, am I home?

Yes, Krong you are home. I can't tell you what happened. All the walls of the years fell away and it felt like we were kids again playing down the street. I opened the door wide so he could pass by me. That's how we began. Simple as that.

We

came in the house and he told me the most incredible story.

Wilema they put me in solitary confinement for ninety days for fighting. You know I was always a warrior. On the fortieth day it happened. A woman came to me in my sleep and said my days of fighting men with my hands was over. Exactly eleven days later a man came to me in my sleep and said that man had always been man even in other worlds. Exactly eleven days after that I just heard a voice. It came in this bright light and it said I was a seedling and I was to bury seeds for the rest of my days and raise them in gardens of plenty. I was told that man was not of the ground but spirit surrounded in a form of time. My whole being was illumined and it scared the guards and everybody. I have had no more fights with men since that day.

Mr. Ulis's

wife died a week after Krong returned and we went to her funeral. The day of her funeral Krong took me next door and knocked on the door of Mr. Ulis's home. When Mr. Ulis opened the door Krong looked at him and then said, I'm sorry for my past behavior. It took me a long time to understand what you meant when you said I didn't have guts. I wasn't man enough then to know when I had gone too far and admit to the person I had trespassed that I was not in my right mind. Thank you for those words they have carried me far.

Mr. Ulis just smiled. It was all any of us needed to say.

Krong

was a barber and I helped him open a shop with some of the money I saved. We got married the third year he was home. He was forty three and I was forty two. We had many children and we had the old neighborhood. I don't have to tell anybody how bad things had gotten. The police shooting people and people shooting police. The growing number of homeless and the foul water. The cost of meat so high many people became involuntary vegetarians. One night Krong woke up screaming and ran out of the house. I chased after him but he disappeared around the corner. He didn't come back home until morning. Coates was with him when he came back. I never seen a man's eyes so distant. I spoke to him but he just walked past me into the house.

Where was he Coates?

He was on 44th street digging in the dirt of an empty lot.

What? I couldn't believe what I was hearing. Did he say anything?

No. I was just driving by when I seen him. I got out my car and ran across the street. I couldn't believe it. He was down on his knees with this branch digging in the dirt…making rows like he was planting crops. I said Krong, what you doing man? Krong! When he finally looked up at me his face had this eerie glow. I tell you Haidu it kinda scared me to see him like that. It was like he didn't see me at all, like he was looking past me at something else.

He got up and his eyes focused themselves on me and he said, We aint got long, a few years, ten no seven. You going to help me aint you Coates? I can't do this alone. I need workers, lots of them. I said, do what Krong? Maybe we should get back to the house and talk about it there.

Then

the police showed up, put a spotlight on us. We knew the one cop that got out of the car with his flashlight pointed at us.

Coates and Krong.

Krong had the branch in his hand and made a move. I saw the eyes of the cop and stepped in front of Krong taking the branch from him. Shoeford this aint nothing but a branch. Krong having some problems as you can see. I was just getting ready to take him home.

Was he digging in the dirt Coates? Your style aint changed but your boy looking like his mind got bent. Think it was all them wars he had inside the steel curtain. Also, heard some strange stories about a light in his cell. You know about that Coates?

Doing time aint no easy thing Shoeford. I wasn't there when the light showed up but he had no more trouble after that, I can tell you that.

Well, get his sick ass home, off the street, yaw both trespassing.

Haidu, you know me, I wanted to put my foot so far in him but I had to get my boy off the street.

Yeah, I know Coates. My name is now Wilema. Krong calls me that. Thanks for bringing him home. I'll stop by in a couple of days, see how he's doing.

The

next day was a long day. Krong woke up after twelve and spent the rest of that day on the computer. The day after that he was at the library all day. Aveka came by and got the keys to open up the barbershop. It was the first time Krong and I did not talk for a solid week. He barely ate. Coates came by several times. On the eighth day I blocked Krong's path and took his hand. I led him out of the house to the porch and we drank lemonade sweetened with ginger syrup.

Are you home Krong?

What.

It's me Wilema, are you home?

It was a long minute before he spoke.

I seen something the other night Wilema, scared me good. I saw people, rail thin and children starving. I saw empty fields with no workers. When the sun came up it was sad and had little heat. And the clouds were moving so fast the rain falling from them landed in the lakes and rivers. The earth was dry and bony. As far as I could see I was the only man standing. You were down on your knees trying to give your tears to a seed sitting on the ground. I started running trying to catch the falling rain but the clouds flew to fast and made it to the horizon before I could catch them. All I had was a tree branch to make rows for the seeds and just kept digging and digging until my fingers were covered with blood. It was not enough and I started to hear the cries of babies and mothers rocking back and forth because there was no more food. I was down on my knees weeping when this old man came across the field and touched me. I looked in his eyes and it was the most peaceful thing I had ever seen. Those clouds took seven years to get there because too much of the earth became barren. There are seeds to be planted, plant them, he said. And he walked out of the field into time.

Of course I just sat there wondering who was this man that was in my house and in my heart. How do I take this in and what are my actions to be? In the face of madness can I take the steps of agreement for more than one day, for more than one year. This word, this message did not come to me. Am I to believe because it sounds heaven sent? How many others have a dream that is just a dream without divine substance?

Krong I don't know what all this means. I can only trust what I have seen and what I have seen is a man that was ambushed by life early in life and that for whatever reason has been chosen to take a step that has moved into the realm of a vision. Those of us like me can't see or feel what has been given to you so all we can do is hope. I believe that something has been communicated to you and so I submit my hand to yours to work in your field.

And so the work began. I remember one special day. We were working in the garden in September. It was late afternoon. Krong and Mr. Ulis both stopped working and walked to the front of the garden and so everybody else stopped working and came to the front of the garden.

The wind is coming Krong do you feel it?

Yes. And Krong's smile made his face bright. The wind came as promised and I listened to it as it came upon us. The wind fell to earth from above and carried my spirit to a place deep within. I closed my eyes along with everybody else and we all heard the wind singing in the voice of a happy child. I curled up in that wind, in that sound and raised myself into joy. The plants were touched by this wind arching themselves to receive this blessing. I now understood the words of the Cry of Beauty: creation is a living language, feel the silent magic, feel the endless warming glo

I don't have to tell you Seso what happened and can only thank you for all the help you gave us. All the homeless people who aided us. And the long journey across the country planting fruit trees. The vine in every yard program and the harvest teams of the teenagers. The idea he had to replace grass with fields of flowers to bring the bees back. And our sixteen children worked with us without too much complaint. Krong helped everyone around us to understand what it meant to be a family again. We were so prepared that even when the earthquakes came and much was lost we had the storehouses to feed the hungry wherever we found them or they found us. Krong said we were workers in the field, you said we were divine farmers working in the heart and soil of the lost. I smile everyday knowing that we did our best.

peace and peace and peace

Wilema

Grandma, I never knew that was how so many people were fed during those horrible times.

Yes, Krong was something special but then god always sends many people to do the work of saving mankind. Whenever a special person is needed, god plants the seed and the people help it to grow even in the midst of suffering. The muscles of courage, to be spiritually strong, are given exercise for the later years to rise into the aura of holiness. No man of god can be a weakling if he is truly going to be a worker in the field of spiritual transmission.

I am now ninety one grandma. I can see now after all these years some of the cycles of life. My life now is so simple not like before when I was young and full of wind. I have a granddaughter who asks me all kinds of questions and you would laugh because now I tell her some of the stories you told me with a few stories of my own. The world I live in is a lot different from yours. I can tell you this she is definitely going to be another worker in the field. She told me the other day that she heard god singing in her heart

THE SUNS APPLE

Rising

from the deepest of sleeps lights of love grasp the new branch of holiness. One of many awakened from the nightmare of ignorance, The Cry of Beauty poured over them the pleasure of balance restored to their world. The winds of life contrasting days of dryness on earth. How many thousands of years passed to fulfill a master plan to remake man again in the image of beauty and wisdom. Man must go down to come up. So, the ancestor speaks from hills of the past in the language of symbols that do not change. The old tree stands taller as the newest branch reaches into the sky of human endeavor seeking to establish new traditions and leaves of its own making.

Hance Charm

came one evening upon Almai. He was among those known as a thief pushed into the alleyway of modern life. They had put upon him that his mouth was too large after he led a rebellion against brutality and suspicion.

I should be able to walk freely in my own neighborhood at any hour, and they came upon him with lies.

We will not be defied, is what was spoken to him and others like him.

These

were the times of the generation after Seso. The fathers of the Greyheads, the children of wisdom. The edifice of the old religions, wine given in large doses based on the suns aperture, were tumbling and the new world was coming into view without a sun as the focal point. The beast of old age used its fingers to claw anything to continue living. Day by day the true thief was losing all that it had stolen and twisted and through the eyes of the new branch of Seso's inheritance water was flowing where once the Vine of the Moon had drunk the water of wine. So many millions laid to rest in graves because of fables and mischief making.

Almai

was a young woman, tears on her face, walking by the Red Lake. She had fallen into the muddy river of sadness. Filled with a madness that had a knife she had only recently removed from her wrist. She had barely been able to defeat the twisted fence loneliness raised around her.

Hance came upon her and together they walked through their anger and loneliness and sadness. They had a common enemy called suffering and they met often until their hearts softened and they could see themselves in each other. Peace, then love joined them together.

One

day they met a Soljah of Seso's at a café and he fed them a portion of what he knew.

Life will not be still, it will go this way or that way. Too much water and it will drown, too little and it will dry up. Use time to find what works for you and remember each life is separate and sacred yet bound to others. Be patient with yourself and others.

Simple

words but words to ponder on and other words from other Soljahs. Blue tipped pearls to gather from this harvest of Seso's suddenly on almost every street corner.

Hance, why have I not heard them before? Almai asked.

I don't think we could have heard them. I have seen them but then my eyes looked out in anger. You have brought me peace and joy. Look in their eye's, peace is the reflection.

And

it was true and the days of Hance and Almai grew in knowing. The house they lived in became a beacon for other's like themselves looking for a way out of misery and the stories of Seso and Octavia and Jake and the sixteen were revealed to them. Then they went to the So'Ya and received the words of the Cry of Beauty and fell headlong into the spirit of HaHiYa. Agony became beauty and the shade of brilliance poured over them. It was clear to them the path their life would take and they began to add more to the earth than they would take away.

How

great is the music of children when they come for no one knows what songs they will sing.

Almai began the urge to manifest in the spring. She took in two seeds from Hance that bore fruit eight months hence. Twins, a boy and girl, Setum and Istum.

Only

HaHiYa cam make suns and worlds, wind and liquids, grasses and animals. Only HaHiYa can bind the eternity of creation. That eye will not open for men, it is the unknown, the mysterious magic never to be shared. We may sail through the galaxies and its distance will remain unknowable no matter the steady drip of wisdom we pull from the ocean of creation, our existence can never be more than a reflection of the permanence of life while our time, even if it reaches into the thousands of years, is only equivalent to one moon floating in space getting its light from a nearby sun. Our children are the ultimate life we can make all else is but copies.

Hance and Almai

took the pamphlets, books, videos and music of Seso to the streets and made their living. They established themselves as merchants of the words of The Cry of Beauty as taught by Seso and the Koba's that lived after him. Riding on the horse of passion left by the spirit of Seso and Octavia they rode deep into the mountain they had left. Taking the reins offered them from the stable of faith stocking their minds with a wagon load of goods they went on the road of the Ocmaba and became Gersoms. They spent a full season in Urton with Setum and Istum, raising themselves as a family Hance and Almai had not known as children. They knew the halfmoon celebration and caught their breath in Mississippi in the winter harvest. Setum and Istum were released on the heart string of HaHiYa through the melodies revealed by Seso, the sounds of HiYa music a source of redemptive joy.

Now

came the first flowers to be raised as Greyheads under the banner of The Cry of Beauty. The streams of Ancestry, Signs & Symbols, and Becoming the branches of learning for the people of the new vine. The Charm family went to school together and learned this way raising themselves as lights to open the door for the generations to follow and the bone of the ancestor had a new way of speaking as the old world passed away. At the age of fourteen Setum and Istum passed into the first stage of Gersom and each was given the Book of Legat to mark their time with commentaries of their own. Hance and Almai were among those that stood at the doorway of becoming Koba's. The years of suffering had provided them with keys not taught in books to see into the hearts of men and women. By chance a neighbor of theirs had a daughter that had been foully treated by her husband, a man said to be mean spirited. At the request of the man's mother Hance was asked to speak with the young man named Pearcy Patt. They met at the Red Lake where the red and white blossoms of spring were in full bloom.

Hance handed the young man a note on which he had written these words:After all the arguing and fighting are done were you closer to your wife or further away? After you pounded on your chest and screamed I am a man and you will do as I say did you win the battle or did the war in your mind go on? For surely this is not a thing of the heart. The children that you have do you kiss them daily and tell them how much you love them? Is there laughter in your house or is the music the sound of human voices in agony?

Then

Hance said to Pearcy, looking him in the eye, Seso once wrote that HaHiYa did not make man to beat on the head of women and children or wage war, he made men as a co-creator. What are you doing to make your days happy days? Everyone loses in war and the land always comes back to what it was when men finish making their mischief. Spring always brings flowers to bloom. Will your family blossom each spring or die because of the bitterness of winter?

Pearcy Patt held his breath as if to burst at the seams. I am undone Hance. I am undone.

And Pearcy ran into the Red Lake. Several men standing way off came running and pulled him from the lake. As he lay there he began to cry. These were the tears of mournfulness, of regret and the pain in each tear was the release of the acid that had eaten down to his bones. Hance, down on one knee, held his hands as Pearcy sobbed uncontrollably. On the other side of the Red Lake a storm was passing, crackling thunder and licking lightening make lasso turns in the sky. Whipping the wind into a frenzy furiously driving the waves of the Red Lake to greater heights. Pearcy Patt placed his head on the bosom of Hance and he rocked him as if he were baby fighting sleep. They spent many hours there and very early in the morning Pearcy awoke. He looked into the eastern sky which was now clear, full of morning stars.

Standing up he felt like a new man. Hance awakened and observed this newness. They looked each other in the eye and there was a knowing words could not express.

Hance said to him, Pearcy come to the Heb, you and your family, you are welcome as I once was to come and be a witness and perhaps even a worker.

Pearcy said to him, I must tell you this, I really do love my wife but it was what an uncle that raised me did to me. I had no father and my mother, my mother, as the old folks say, every woman is not a mother and she wasn't and she just left us at home one day. My uncle abused me and then disappeared leaving us with no money, my sisters and brothers. There were nine of us and the oldest was fifteen, my brother Det. He tried to take care of us but he got killed trying to rob a store. My brother under him Jatel and my oldest sister Shenah started selling drugs to keep the family together after Det died. Man, there was always somebody arguing or hungry or crying. I swore I would never treat kids like that but I think I was carrying a whole lot of anger against women because of my momma. I was bitter, so bitter, so angry and my wife, which I didn't realize when I married her, looked just like my momma, even act like her. She always wanted to go somewhere. One day we was arguing and I asked her why she always wanted to be gone from the house, away from the kids and away from me, and she yelled at me because when she was a kid her grandfather wouldn't let her go anywhere and at night would lock her in a room that didn't have no window. I was so messed up with my own stuff I never really thought about how that could hurt a person until last night that's why I ran into the lake. I wanted to die. Pearcy's eyes filled again with tears. Go home to your wife, you have much to talk about. Don't be ashamed of the tears, sometimes there is no other way to come up than to go down.

Pearcy Patt again left Hance running only this time he went up the road not into the lake.

A woman, sick with a disease that wracked her skin and body produced a sour odor. But she was stronger than the doctors and after they sent her home to die she listed left and right like a boat on a violent sea but she rode on top of the waves and would not be pulled under.

There was much barking between the family and the husband, who many said had abandoned his wife and many evenings when they thought he should have been at home he was nowhere to be found. Low came the voice of suspicion from her aunt, maybe the boy got another woman stashed on the other side of town somewhere. Rising one day the sick woman found her way to the store and back. Coming by to visit her a sister came upon her in the driveway with a bag of candy bars.

How'd you get out here in the driveway and what you got in that bag? You been to the store? the sister yelled raising an alarm.

Out of the house came another sister and brother. Where you going with her? the brother said looking at the sister that had come upon the sick woman in the driveway.

I aint going nowhere with her. When I drove up she was standing in the driveway with that bag in her hand?

Bag? You been to the store Ilre? You too sick to go to the store.

Why you trying to do this, you trying to kill us with worry?

No, I just wanted to get outside and feel some air. I been telling yaw but yaw wasn't listening. Everybody trying to tell me, I still got my mind, knows what I want. Ilre knows what she doing.

What you got in that bag, Ilre?

Candy, want some? and Ilre took the bag and dumped the candy on the ground and went in the house. The three siblings stood there in amazement. They decided to wait and talk to her husband when he got home. Very early in the morning they heard voices outside. Two men entered the house. The two sisters and brother rose up as one and faced the two men. lre's husband Thomfield Spencer was slow to anger but was known as fearless once riled.

Your wife was out buying candy today? said Ilre's sister Crateria, an exaggerator. We called your cell phone but you never answered. And she leaned back on her heels with a hand on hips.

Hance this is my wife's sisters and brother. Everybody this is Hance Charm, Thomfield said not responding to the news he just heard. He was a child born when the moons light was receding. Did you hear what we said, your wife, my sister Ilre was outside. She walked down to the corner store and bought a bag of candy! Ilre's brother was the shortest man in the family and had the most money. Juba Kilner owned two cleaners and a small restaurant that served breakfast and a variety of greens and bean soups, sandwiches, salads and homemade biscuits.

Where were you? How'd she get out the house? Thomfield said.

How do I know I was on the phone with my accountant. Crateria was upstairs with her I was in the family room.

No, I wasn't, I was in the basement washing clothes. I didn't know nothing until I heard you running across the floor over my head and then I ran up the steps and saw you go out the side door. She musta' went out while we was busy.

That ain't what's important, it's over now. We got the candy and she back in bed where she belongs.

The more practical of the sisters Patreast said taking her turn. We stayed so we could talk to you. There's a rumor going around that you are seeing another woman and that you just waiting for our sister to die so you can have your time.

The accusation hit Thomfield so hard he lost his balance. Hance used his body to shore him up.

You think I don't love my wife? Have you looked at her, what's become of her?

Crateria glared at him, then where you been all these nights not coming home until all hours of the morning and nobody here to watch over our sister?

Somebody is here every night watching over her until I get here.

Ain't nobody been over here tonight?

I know she called me and told me you were here.

Who called you?

The lady across the street, her and Ilre went to cosmetology school together, comes over when nobody is here. She's not married and has no children.

Isn't that that blind lady? Juba protested. How that lady gone watch anybody?

She has a special gift, Thomfield replied evenly.

Wait a minute this is getting off the subject, Crateria charged, What we want to know is where you at till all hours of the morning?

Hance took a step forward and said, He's been with me.

I know who you are, you down there with that group that followed that man Seso. Yaw got a place called The Heb, a kind of a church or something. Patreast said. What kind of religion is that anyway where don't nobody get baptized or saved. My pastor told us all about what yaw do down there. Patreast was deeply religious and judgmental.

We don't follow a religion, a believe system, for us the path is a way of life but that is not what this is about is it?

What I do is nobody's business. If you all hadn't been here Mr. Charm would not have known any of this about my wife's illness. He only suspected but he would not pry or turn dirt like you seem to do.

Turn dirt! That's a foul thing for you to be saying. She's our sister and she dying and nothing nobody can do about it. But she deserves to pass in a graceful way without a lot of back dealing and sneaking go on behind her back.

You want to talk about sneaking and back dealing what about the way your family tried to get her moved out of our house to your sister's house over in Akon on the other side of Red Lake. Or wanting to know who was the beneficiary on her insurance policy and how much it was? What about what church was to preside over her home going. Oh yeah, yaw been turning some dirt and asking questions about things that don't concern you. And worst of all you been pointing fingers and casting lines of suspicion over everything I do. Well, it aint nobody's business. I'm her husband and for your information I do love her, always have and always will.

Listen, I know you mean well but to clear this up, like I said, Thomfield has been with me. He came by The Heb one day said a friend had sent him over. We got a farm out in Urton and we needed some help with some improvements we were making. Thomfield agreed to help out. His car broke down tonight and that's why I'm here.

So, that's why nobody saw you around? Patreast said.

If you had trusted me in the first place that would never had been necessary, Thomfield said taking a seat. They all set down.

A week later Ilre died. Patreast came to The Heb to see Hance.

Why did you convince Thomfield to have my sisters' home going here. Yaw don't believe in saving souls and baptizing.

Baptism

is not of the water and the soul is a life of great beauty. Seso revealed that the sun is not a savior but an old story of great symbolism to throw light on the path for the growth of man spiritually. It is the symbols of wisdom that we use to seek HaHiYa in ourselves and in all we see. Creation is a lliving language and it spins. Everything in creation is in orbit of something grander than itself. Change one perspective and everything changes, a blue sky to orange or one sun to two. Would then men say that saviors come in pairs and that this is his son and daughter or son and son or daughter and daughter? What are the limits of creation? I have seen none except those that men frame and I have not witnessed any final thing except those that men declare. And men have used these declarations of finality to enslave the minds of men and women. Seso gave witness to a new vision of creation that was not fenced in by the past fables or mysticism. HaHiYa gave him a breeze of life and it filled him all his days and it flowed to Octavia and Jake and Samala and Fidance and the others. No, I did not ask for Ilre's body to preside over it nor did I ever offer Thomfield anything but he came on his own.

What are we supposed to do? I can't come here for her home going, Patreast said frustrated.

Why can't you come, you came here now pointing your finger at me just like you did Thomfield. I bear you no harm or anger. Unlike Thomfield I'm asking you for the sake of your family unball the fist that is in your mind and come.

Thomfield Spencer

spared no expense in the arrangements for his Ilre's home going. The Heb which was already a physically beautiful building with its waterfall and raised dais. The arena seating and colorful decorations of nature abounding. He had almost no contact with his wife's family since that night almost two weeks ago and they even came at different hours to view the body. The blind lady across the street said she had seen that the family was very angry at him for having Ilre's final remarks being given at The Heb, which they considered to be heresy. She saw other things as well, like when Ilre would pass from this world to the next and she saw Thomfield leaving this world not more than six months later, killed by a tree on a farm, which she couldn't identify at that time. She saw a tall man with a charm standing over him with tears in his eyes. The man turned out to be Hance Charm who had just walked away when the tree, weakened by a recent week of steady rain just fell down.

Thomfield

set alone in the front row of seats reserved for the family. The choir had rose to sing when the doors opened on the west side of the church and Ilre's brothers and sisters and all the Kilner family piled in. Eighty-nine souls of family, each of them led by Patreast came and hugged their brother n law and viewed their sisters remains. The choir produced a moving song of HiYa music that had The Heb rocking in great spiritual salutation. Even the entire visiting Kilner family could not resist the infectious rhythms and voices calling out refrains so moving it raised the ancestors of Khamit. It was as if the many fractured parts of the past had come together at last to celebrate a reunion of being one again.

At the end of the song Hance came to the edge of the dais and spoke.

Seso

spoke once of a thing he called The Suns Apple. Seso spoke often about the profound symbolism of creation. According to his son Republic he made the following observation:

HaHiYa placed the angle of the sun and its satellite's in positions that would give us endless wisdom. That creation was a textbook that we could learn from without destroying it because it was so far beyond our reach the only thing we could do is dwell upon it in wonder. He give this speech in the sign of Leo which is the highpoint of the sun, when its rays are strongest. Seso said that if one has a keen spiritual imagination then much can be gleaned. The Cry of Beauty reveals that creation is a lliving language and all of creation speaks the same language and it is divine when once you see it and then hear it. The rays of HaHiYa come through the other world by way of his ambassadors and our souls become the witness. Now you might be wondering what does any of this have to do with the celebration of a loved one that has passed on. It is to let all men know that living and dying is not the province of any religion but the claim that HaHiYa has on all that he has created. There is no religion or savior that has any words for the passing on of a single leaf or a sun in a distant galaxy. How much more is the passing of a man than that of a sun without whose light the living would dwell in eternal darkness. Seso observed that there was much spiritual symbolism in the garden of HaHiYa. The work one does in this world continues on in the next. It is the soul's inspiration that revives us daily to march on until the body can do no more or because of accidents and human errors.

Is not man the sun's apple in this garden of delight we call living? Are we not the copying architects of all that we see. Is our building incessant and do we not make the rules by which we govern ourselves and our nations? This is all a reflection of the soul and this is the portion that we can understand. In that casket lies the body of Ilre Spencer but she is now living on as the soul she always was. She has been born again in the world she knew before this one.

HaHiYa unfolds his mysteries here and there without end. Life on earth has its termination point. The body will go down and not rise again. Living is a war, a struggle against all the things that cause restlessness, keeps us from knowing peace. Tiny, insignificant little things. Coming into us like worms, so small they seem to have no purpose other than to burrow and aerate. Without moisture or cover caught in the rays of the sun these worms would shrivel and die. Seso writes there is great symbolism here.

Seso said that in the soul of man is a fruit bearing tree that grows without end. That this tree is fed by a river of love. That the water is so pure it shines. Sister Ilre must have come upon this river of love and followed it to a standing pool and took a sip and it was so sweet she sat there for a long time just sipping it until she was full. And she noticed how much the water tasted like an apple and so she got up and followed the river to its source and came upon a field of giant apples fermenting under the sun of god. The river was the nectar from the apples flowing on the ground. The acid in the nectar prevented the worms from infecting the trees in the field. It is the same with a man or woman of HaHiYa entering into the field of spiritual relevance. As you grow spiritually the body is fermenting as is the heart as is the mind all trying to reach the nectar of the soul.

The river of love is what drove Ilre that day to get out of her bed and get some candy. So strong was the spirit that it raised her body from that bed to reach for something that she had experienced in her soul. She wanted to taste the sweetness of life that she saw in her soul. Seso said too many times people listen to the worms gathering about the tree of life and let the worms in to their minds and into their hearts where they fester and foment and agitate themselves and others, infecting life around them with diseases. Ilre has travelled over to the other side where she can continue to taste the sweetness of the sun's apple, where she can continue her journey into gods places and worlds of understanding and joy. She is not the body of the sun nor has she gone after the body of the sun.

Those of us that are among the living must be mindful of the worms of life. That they do seek us out to join with us to turn dirt and other things pretending to be in fashion when in reality they bring dark clouds to cover us with a blanket of diseases. The Suns Apple is in a valley, a flat plain or even a mountain top. The Suns Apple is anywhere you are if you but knew it. And when you taste its nectar you will come again and again and sip until you are full. Seso was the Suns Apple and his nectar was love. As I have drank his nectar, which is to say his wisdom, I have come often to the river of his love and put my face in its water to gather the treasures HaHiYa gave him to give to us.

Hance Charm and Almai raised their children in the river of the Suns Apple and when they were grown they too followed the pathway of the Ocmaba and also became Koba's of The Cry of Beauty.

Patreast Kilner in her old age claimed to have seen a vision of her sister eating apples and gave her a bite. She said it was the sweetest apple she had ever tasted. They walked together to a nearby building and she saw a man and woman with long dreadlocks. One day walking by one of the soljahs of Seso she saw the man and woman on the cover of a book he was selling. When she found out who it was she went down to The Heb and became one of its member. She was one of its biggest advocates before she left this world at the age of ninety four.

BOOK OF SPLENDOR

1.

1. *You*
2. weep for your pets
3. you weep for the death of love ones
4. Be Silent and Listen
5. Let me tell you something unimaginable
6. How many on how many worlds weep
   for the death of a sun?
7. There is no creation if there are no suns.

2.

1. Let me introduce you to the clever mankind
2. The robber has stolen from the family
3. The dictator destroys the children
4. kills by the thousands and millions
5. The rules of man create upheaval and wars
6. The minds of these men leaving this world
7. with the same thoughts they came to the world.
8. So this is what mankind does with free will?
9. Others sit silent watching evil intent grow
10. Afraid of entering the fray
11. Others cheer nastiness

12. thinking thoughts of participation
13. the spoils of oppression
    counted on their living room floor
14. All of these minds like fish in the sea
    the big one eats the little ones
15. There are other clever men and women
16. human bondage a wager on the street
    houses of commerce slicing livers full of emotion
17. retail sales lies to capture the mind and empty pockets
18. politicians with double minds and even more tongues
19. Once they were babies without thoughts
20. At what age did they awaken in this world?
21. Their minds a treasure chest full of tricks and treats
    delighted with themselves
22. If the mind suffered much because
    the body wracked with pain
23. If the body was beaten starved made sick
24. If the emotions needed emergency care
25. or were trotted around on a lease
    troubled in childhood set upon by night
    made to go fearful in the day
    wrestling with adults seeking young warm bodies
26. even wonderful minds intent on saving the world
    get into the drain of drama
27. all flushed into the same river seeking salvation
    or relief or just a moment of peace
28. Be Silent and listen

3.

1. All
2. that has been done is written in the Book of Splendor.

3. It is the book of light

   even the faded light of the wicked.

4. It is the mind you came with

5. It is the mind you leave with

6. This document of creation is the word

7. I

8. have sent my agents to have a private word with you

9. some loudly

10. some quietly

11. some just whisper

12. If you were made to obey

   what kind of creation would that be?

13. My suns have space from their worlds.

14. My galaxies have space from one another

15. My celestial gardens spin.

16. The asteroids are the remains of the death

   of some of my stars worlds

17. Asteroids are the death of some worlds

   destroyed by men wise and unwise.

18. Those new to travel will not believe these things

   imagining themselves as lonely

19. Not knowing how old their minds really are.

20. The awakening called genius

   unaware that the time had come

21. Just like this *Book* could not exist to them before today

22. Man speaks of his vision

23. how the universe is expanding?

24. It spins.

25. Some galaxies in small circles

   other sweeping elliptical turns

26. moving across one another

    through others   dancing stars

27. Exchanging Suns like electrons

28. no one calls it stealing   no one can

4.

1. Be Silent and Listen

2. Do you know that creation has roots just like a tree?
    Space is the soil of creation

3. Close your eyes and look.

4. See in that space light

5. See in that space your imagination

6. See you looking at you.

7. The road Wonderful
    is on the other side of the door

8. It is time that opens it.

9. Ignorance and fear keep it closed

10. The most ragged man in the world gave away his life

11. the world either too big or too small

12. The rich man gave away his life
    anchored to silver and gold

13. Men and women give away their life
    lost under the hammers of control

14. False preachers lie about fire and brimstone
    and a world to come that never existed

15. Do you really think that the mind and
    habits you brought with you came from hell?

16. How much different you are
    from your brothers and sisters

17. Unique among your friends

18. Not something that could happen overnight

19. Man has no concept of eternity

20. Man has no concept in which direction

    creation ends or begins

21. Man only knows the world he lives in

    while he lives in it.

5.

1. We
2. could give you images to make you weep
3. fill your hearts with strings of music
4. make a flower of beauty grow in space
5. beds of celestial gardens full of stories
6. flow through the face to make it glorious
7. add color to water without making you drunk
8. letting you know that each sun

    is just another drop of the Creator

9. living life as it was meant to be
10. talk about the making of words
11. symbols alive in the mind active as free will
12. to go anywhere at anytime
13. but men have a desire
14. not like bees to make honey for the nest
15. many animals and insects kill for a living

    my planets erupt and shake themselves

    my rivers overflow their banks

16. when men know these things why do they build

    where I do my work?

17. How many men would guide a ship into space

    where suns are exploding?

18. Where is the mind of man?
19. When are those, who have been silent, speak?
20. You are more than them, where is your voice?

21. Have the silent ones not learned
    a raucous noise has to be quieted?
22. How can the quiet ones think or
    have peace when they opened the door
    for suffering to occur?
23. Sitting by the door peeking out
    hoping they will not be dragged out into the open.
24. The minds of all that live will leave this world
    with whatever state of mind they are in.
25. Did you seek to make the world safe?
26. Did you try to make happiness?
27. Were you a witness to *Good* and *Evil* and did nothing?
28. Who told you to obey them and you did?

6.

1. The Book of Splendor
2. is over filled with the wonders of Creation
3. HaHiYa's name is there
4. His spread of delights
    the food he offers to visiting souls
5. When *You* find yourself come to his table
6. a *Creation* that you could not have known before
    awaits you
7. join with others who have travelled
    past the Day of Separation
8. whose minds are now one mind
9. whose day is now one day
10. whose life bows in reverence
11. who is a Sun to all in their company
12. they see the horrors men create

13. know that the robber is the child of ignorance and fear
14. the dictators anger looking for someone to love
    that doesn't love him
15. should we show them how to pray
    or wait for salvation
16. creeping through generations to their pores
17. the blood of so many nations
    leaking into roots of plants
18. Battlefields disappearing under the march of nature
19. so what did men win?
20. even in times of peace
    too many people gather in small places
21. now there are too many strangers
22. and too many neighborhoods
23. and too many buildings
24. and not enough roads
25. and not enough work
26. even in peace ignorance and fear
    have seats at the head of the table
27. the work of greed a slippery show
28. another state of mind adventurous in the world
29. and again the silence of those who could object
30. quieted by the noise of pointing fingers and ink pens
31. rejecting the images of artists
32. reshuffling music to satisfy the taste of the rich
33. making certain that certain poets do not have fame
34. taking hold of an agent that might have a following
35. but full of fear if one rises up and speaks *Divinely*
36. the mind of one who has journeyed
    into the world of peace
    cannot be leveled

37. that one is not of this world or its assets

38. the mind once having seen the splendor of light

39. cannot be deceived

40. can be mocked but not turned

41. the scene of earth war torn

    small hills of men with their light cocked

    flying the flag of the Cry of Beauty

42. a still shot on the clock of events

43. by what motivation would shadows gather an army

44. on what border of infamy to cross the line

45. Believing that they are only seen in this world

    and not the other

46. changing the names of things

    as if that would erase the past

47. making simple documents to imprison resistors

48. making farmers and engineers

    and politicians and preachers

    assistants in fattening their tables

49. never mind they say to the Sun

    I am the true light of day and I bring salvation

7.

1. The Book of Splendor calls out to all

2. It is a moment of wonder

3. it has a *Sun* in it

4. it has you in it

5. the root of you tapping into a body of light

6. Some say the ancestors live here with you

7. Some say this is the place where souls fly from

8. Some say many things   magical things

9. brought to life by chants and incantations

10. how will you know if you only listen to others?

10. it is your mind to command

11. after many days of pondering

    all the storms firing scene after scene slowly fade away

12. an image of peace forms inside the now still mind

13. On a night when the Moon stops changing shape

14. When the Sun stops moving   when all of nature pauses it comes to you to choose

15. not on a horse but on wings of silence

    of the Cry of Beauty

16. quietly stealing You away

17. laying you on a river of peace

18. from which you have no desire to rise

19. this mind if you can hold it is a magnet

20. making all the little things whole

21. setting aside the trips of misery

22. on the mantle a orb of glory shines

23. inside the mirror in the background of your life

24. how much more can we reveal to you Man

    to make you see

25. what about your little wars

    compared to meteors of ancient destruction

26. ripping through cosmos destroying planets and moons

27. what about your words and music

    of wisdom and beauty

28. can any of you hear the music of a single galaxy?

29. or match the wisdom of one spinning atom?

30. all that is here is Lessons   go to school

31. your tools of destruction are not envied

32. spin the mind on what is before you

    carefully to avoid dizziness

33. my divine ones are not weak

    they are just being patient

34. they give out jewels sprayed with the oil of genius

35. to awaken those that have prepared themselves

    to wake up

36. Come with us when you are tired of all this

    when you seek a better way

37. when you get tired of looking at yourself as you are

38. unlike blue skies or mountains

    or oceans or sand or stars

39. you never get tired of looking at the beauty of creation

40. because it is Beautiful and it never stops   never pauses

41. and it is wise   composes in every way

    every idea of wisdom we will ever know

42. The mind now is at attention   your opportunity

  to take control and be a loving guide

8.

1. Lastly, we say when the Sun's Goat reaches the summit

    it rests for three days

2. Then rises early to begin a journey

    down to the valley of delights

3. Those special ones who reach the summit

    are at their weakest point

4. exposed to the world when a suckling babe

    new to that world

5. hurry to them with shields and clothe them

    so that they are not known

6. At it is written in Travelling to the Word

    those in darkness

7. will go anywhere to conduct their business

8. know that these men have a master

9. know that these men also have a god that they follow

10. believing that this god lives in the shadows of things

11. works magic and protects them and rewards them in this world and the next

12. living in the ignorance of the One Law

13. living in ignorance of the balance of the flowers

    receiving light are more than they

14. Seso

15. showed the way and all that went with him in his time

    and after him came others

16. There is no fear in his people and

    they do not turn their back to enemies

17. Accept no invitations to be trod upon

18. The soldiers of Seso were not blades of grass

    but stout limbs on a strong tree

19. Abukan bees too take flight and

    wage a hearty contest if that is the request

20. But not all men are warriors

21. The people of HaHiYa give much charity and

    repair at the end of a conflict

22. work to smile and converse with neighbors

    near and far

23. making all aware that they nor their children are fools

24. Man make way for the woman to have her voice and position without opposition

25. how simple this living could be

    if peace were sought instead of violations

26. The truth is that Lessons are needed and

    nature and animals and men are the subjects

27. While you meditate in silence

    establish regimens for you and the family

28. Be strong and be wise

29. It is the creation you live in

    not heaven or some other idea of joy

30. Creation was made in Time

31. It yawns and it screams   it plays and it storms

    it whispers and it sings   it creeps and it flies

32. Go among the created without fear

    but never fear to hesitate

    listen to the heartbeat of it

33. The road on which man travels

    is full of curves and parallels

34. One day it comes to a crossroad

35. The inquirer ask which way do I go

36. We all know once the step is taken

    even if taken back   everything has already changed

37. at the crossroad a decision has been made

38. The event or person to meet or have met

39. To go on with the event or person or not go

40. Once on our own father and mother

    talk less to us daily or weekly

41. once out of sight we become

    our own branch

    our own tree

42. We must find soil to root in

43. we must find an orbit to circle the sun

44. receive our daily bread

45. love someone have children have friends and create

46. fight with our selves work out in the field of ignorance

    aware as we get old how little we know

47. Come to a place where our god lives and listen

48. This is the life we have chosen

49. Surely man knows that this is not an accident of birth

50. the mother and the father and brothahs

    and sistahs and friends   husbands and wives

51. the Cry of Beauty of all this

    singing through all our days and nights

52. peace and wisdom given in doses

53. Be silent and listen if you can

54. You are coming for you

55. You are the Sun's Goat

56. You are going into your own valley of delights

    brush aside the shadows and walk in the light of

     HaHiYa

    and know its sweetness

    the water smiles in creation

THE FOUR LIGHTS

FROM THIS SPOT

The
video began and I saw Seso speaking for the first time. There was nothing surprising in what I imagined he was like if I could have been in his presence. He could only have looked this way. Eyes of abiding peace, steady and inviting. His physical size residing in poise ready to move in the direction of HaHiYa. His voice, a steady chant, a drumbeat calling the heart, the spirit to awaken and follow where his steps were going without hesitation. Seso was living love. These were his words delivered that day:

From
this spot I go forward. From this spot all of creation goes forward. The one was always two. Female and Male. God as creator was never one. Creation is the marriage of a man and woman. The smallest atom is made of a nucleus and an electron and men decided that positive is masculine and negative is feminine.

One
hundred and thirty years ago From This Spot there were no cars. One thousand years ago From This Spot this land was home to black and red men and women whose children did not know the meaning of the word jail. Seventeen thousand b.c. Abukans sailed across the sea and settled in what we call today South America. Hundreds of thousands of years ago men grew in consciousness and began to dominate the land. Somewhere in time wise beings traveled through the galaxy and peopled worlds before the sun that shines on us ever existed. It is not in the realm of possibility that humans living here never existed before and that we are alone, some unique form in creation. We are not unique and we are not the only ones that know what it means to be alive and to change the face of the world we live on. The law of Abundance says there has never been one of anything. Not one sun but endless numbers of them.

In
the House of Creation there was never one of anything. Light could be feminine and dark could be masculine. There can be no y without an x but only the x can carry the child. The Law of Abundance is the original witness for if there was no addition there could not be subtraction and the many have always been more than the few. Creations balance is more not less. When the weaver prepares to make a coat of skins, it is made of many feet of yarn yet once sewn it appears with arms and a front and back and a collar, and depth. Man appears as a front and back, a top and a bottom and depth. The sum of man is the same as creation and that number is five. All that exists in creation has a unique space, one from another and the distance is time. The wind of creation blows everywhere causing friction and friction is fire. How can darkness come alone when fire exists everywhere?

Which
child of man said god was a man? Did not all the children, male and female come from the womb of a woman? The forms of creation born from an endless womb birthing and dying in celestial gardens, sucked down into faceless blackholes, burping portions of their remains onto the soil of space. The House of Creation moves in one direction. Atoms whirl, spinning into molecules; molecules whirl into spectacular amalgamations making suns, suns spin and spew gases that spin into worlds.

Earth
bound scientist and religious sages seek to know when did conscious beings begin? Where does this creation that we can see begin? Where is the spot that is the end and a veil exists, under space of some unknown matter or how many levels does the soil of space go that no tool of man can see into or beyond like the cloak of death that hides itself in a cocoon of the dead waiting for a

resurrection to live again on earth? All any of us know is this life in the moments and years we have them. We do not know what the tree thinks after one thousand years of tossing out oxygen for man to breathe or the turtle alive for over two hundred years coming out of the ocean a witness to the work of mankind.

The
child comes to the circle of imagination and is told it has limits. Another child, motherless and fatherless, is said to be a runner, cannot be tamed. History is the witness, the story keeper of many famous men and women that tossed aside the measuring stick of their time and walked into the wilderness of the imagination and discovered jewels of wonder lying about. Some say it was their destiny, that it was divine. Each of us one day awakened in this world, whether we had brothers or sisters or mothers and fathers, the mind that we knew the world with never left us, remaining the same touched by experience and the limits put there by traditions of the day. When men wanted to change the world war was the common pathway. Kings or emperors pretending to be inheritors of gods power taking thousands and millions into the battlefield of darkness.

From This Spot,
as it was in the past, creation flows into a flower blooming in the sunrise of endless tomorrows. For each sun born in the celestial gardens of creation a child is born here and on many worlds. The House of Abundance is the child's abode. Limited only by what can be imagined. The child comes to the edge of the imagination where there are no forms only endless space. There is no sound, silence has placed sound in a corner. The child knows the limits of its feet, its legs, its hands, its arms, its tongue, its eyes, and its ears. The physical world of wood and stone and gases flipped on their edge and operated on by tools created from the imagination. But where is the machine that can advance the imagination into the beyond? Beyond life? There is none.

From This Spot in our imaginations, we can only be a witness and wonder at how limitless we can be.

There
are those caught in the net of materialism and history. They are not fishermen seeking the sea of revelation. The waters they walk on are shallow and limited with schemes and narrow messages to make men kings and others their servants. They have allowed themselves a few hundred thousand years tied to this earth and no other. Imagining the earth as a jail cell where all men had their beginning and a long night of original sin. Alone in a creation still trying to find ways to trick each other paying weekly tributes to forgive sins set down in books, setting limits on what is and what is not a sin.

From This Spot
There is another side. Where there is surely light. Abundant light. The imagination is the tool to slip inside the veil. Quiet the noise of the mind, fold the body and put it aside. There was a time before earth had man and animals and plants. The journey of life certainly billions of years old and repeated over and over. That which we have come to know is because it existed before.

What
we call history is not limited to the stories we pass on. Wisdom is not the sole province of man. Is not light wisdom? If there were no Suns there would be no life. Wrapped in the Sun are zillions of atoms originally molecules we call hydrogen. The architectural arrangement of creations design is wisdom itself. Stars become man exciting man to question existence. Creation is a lliving language talking every moment. Creation causes us to speak. It is the House of limits that make man think we alone speak. Colors sprinkled across the heavens give us beauty. There is no remark of being tired of creation. There is no empty breadbasket in the cupboard of creation as it flies about spinning gold and helium and nitrogen and oxygen weaving the fabric of suns. This is creation.

The House of Wings.

From This Spot   From any Spot this is creation.

Alive with man. Alive without man.
Suns
with worlds without man alive. Living and dying with no human or conscious being like man. Not a single human whisper yet they live and die. There are weeds in the garden and there is bountifulness. Come and see. The witness sees what is there and listens. Some trees are knarled, beat up by storms and mudslides. Other trees are so majestic they appear to have the beauty of the eyes of female deer or the sheer magnitude of the mountains looking over their shoulder. All admit to the wisdom trees impart: roots for food like the ancestors stories; trunks like houses to keep the family warm; and branches multiplying like a family today raising children for tomorrow. Trees always follow the light of the sun and give of their bounty without judgement or reward.
We
are the substance of timelessness, the essence of sweetness existing in the imagination of creation. Consciousness that gave breathe to the living for a moment to be a witness to good and evil and choose a path either to raise the light or chop at its flame.
I
Seso, stand before you all as a living man in a living creation not dead anywhere. The state of Becoming transfigured on the cross we all bear. Not immaculately conceived but raising ourselves on the narrowest pathway imaginable to shed our ways for the salvation of our souls. Only I can save me. Only I can resurrect me. Only I can see the light of creation for myself. We walk together and inspire together and observe together but the work of being the witness of HaHiYa has to be done by the seeker.
Is
this not how each of us came into this world. Pushed into existence by a mother. Fed in the womb, a watery cave fed by a tube. And then suddenly freed, awakened by oxygen, to have the experience of the troubles of life, to become the witness of nature, wood, oil, stone and metal, transformed by the imagination of mankind. How long have these forms existed in creation and who was their maker?
From This Spot
all this has lived before, existed before. As our consciousness grows we discover that which was. It is on the road of abundance we see the jewelry of the techniques of creation and marvel at its simplicity and its profound wisdom and beauty.
It
is no wonder when we realize something we smile. Is that not what the animal does when they are alone with the family and play. Even the lion knows how to smile. It is that smile that is in every atom in creation. How else do you think we know to do it? How could you have not known the smile of atoms. They have the oldest memories of all and they tell us stories of wonder when we are quiet and listen.
I am smiling From This Spot
The Cry of Beauty has moved into my heart brought there by the vision creation has made.

THE BOOK OF BOOKS

Creation is not impatient
each atom as fresh as the moment it flowered
eternal travelers
each a living word announcing the newness of all forms
How is it then that men consider themselves alone?
A baby sun on the edge of a galaxy disc
A galaxy with dying suns burning in space
trillions of galaxies old and new and some yet born
Creation could create suns but not men?
Spin worlds with oceans and living things but not men?
Listen to this revelation man
You are not new to this creation.
The memory of the journeys of the created written
under the face of living skin

1.

In
the past there was no beginning anyone could see.
The oldest galaxy of beings remembered was Arapes
they passed into legend billions of years ago
known only by the words traced on the womb
of the awakened ones dispersed through the
galaxy of Pix
Few remembered Ethe for he was the light
What he knew he gave to the Drex young warriors that fell upon many until they came upon the Lims
The Lims lived on the most beautiful world in the
Galaxy Pix
It was the ancestral world of the oldest beings in Pix
some said they carried the seed of Arapes
Among the Drex was one born with knowledge of decrees
Landing on Lim the light opened deeper in his soul
One called Onay went before him and saw his light
Kram come with me before the circle
there you will behold the manifestation
And Kram walked in the oldest way
This wisdom always exists, the seeker needing a hand
male and female sat in the circle like sunfire
Onay made the words spin as the creation spins
Kram looked deep into the book of creation
After the passage of many years his
eye opened

He spoke the words of life
He walked with the words of life
He took the ship of his people and journeyed to many worlds
The Drex no longer were a warrior people
They carried the seed of life before they too
passed into legend
Now came the Olians
They were merchants traveling through Pix
Word came to them of a traveler from the disk galaxy
They took themselves and met with these beings
The youthfulness of them abounded as they were new
to traveling through space.
The Olians helped with their ship and promised to
journey with them in ships of light.
The Olians were descendants of the Drex and the Lims
They were enlightened but defended themselves
with classes of warriors
They ruled with government meeting in councils
Meeting the beings of the disk galaxy they raised
them to a level unknown to them.
One day the female among them, Udi,
came before them and asked their age
The Olian Pock said to her that he did not know, that it was in the millions of years.
It was not something that Udi could believe.
We have studied the heavens, its stars, its galaxies and have our awakened ones. We have not this knowledge.
And
your ships that brought you here are hundreds slower than ours. Your ship carries seven hundred beings. We have ships we call Zarkans that carry twenty five thousand beings and five thousand animals. We stock them with seeds and plants from many worlds. We have taken ourselves to empty worlds a million or more years ago and populated them with ourselves and others. What is your believe to us when we see you as new to these things that you did not know before. We don't have your belief's because we know.
Udi came to her people with this news and many sat quiet
Soon the day came for them to leave to go back home.
Will you send some of your people with us as a guide and show us some of what you know about traveling through space as fast as you do.
Pock said, you can travel back on one of our smaller ships. What is years journey to you will only take one of your years.

2.

Travel
between galaxies was not new to the Olians. In just one year they were back in their own galaxy, a disc spinning sideways. Now these people, known as Seria, came with the Olians and were taught by them. And the things made known were written in the Book of Books. When the Olian left to return home they left the admonishment to Serians to care for all that they found in their own galaxy and raise them up as they had been raised but only in due time. That worlds found suitable go to them and make deposits of plants and animals so that life can go on beyond their own days.

After many years the Serians journeyed throughout their galaxy and made deposits of plants and animals on worlds found suitable to life. After hundreds of thousands of years, the mighty of some worlds came into powers. Rulership of the galaxy came into conflict between the old and the new. Wars seen in ancient minds had seen these events in the galaxies of the Arapes and Pix. The words of the Book of Books had no meaning for the rising warrior worlds seeking power. They took for themselves this world and that making heavy threats and alliances.

The Serians having knowledge of ancient events sent a ship to the edge of the galaxy to a young star to the fourth planet. On the ship was placed the Book of Books with all the history of what was known by the Olians both good and bad. It was the Tree which the Olians said gave them light and fed their souls. It was the guide of refreshment for when the world gets old and the time for its people to move on if they are to live.

The deposit was made according to the laws that the Serians had inherited. After thousands of years differences rose up among the people and some of them migrated to a nearby world for peace. Yet, as before some cannot be satisfied with a partial score. The weapons of war laid eyes on their enemies and sought to destroy them. The silent stones orbit the sun to this day. Few escaped on either world falling from space onto the third world from the sun.

Billions of years ago this world had been too hot to occupy. Slowly as it cooled it was one of the world that the Drex of Pix had made deposits of plants and then animals from many worlds to make their way. Many of these animals were little more that small cells that would thrive or die in the water or on land. A minority of eggs of flying animals were deposited later. And so for more than five hundred million years no one had visited and it was lost in time nor written in any book or spoke of in any circles of beings.

Those that fell upon this world came as the first beings to call it home and subdue it. To name the plants and animals. To make time and give this world a language of understanding and create history where there was none before. After many generations all knowledge of what had gone before was lost to many except for the Keepers of the Book of Book.

Although they had not the book they had the words of the ancient ones:

>they have come before this Sun to be born male and female
>they have come to multiply their wisdom
>standing under this tree before the Mighty Ones
>we have sent them words that they might obey
>stray not from this path and go among the pathless
>make no fires for people to burn themselves
>know that one day a kin of ours will return to give you the light you have lost
>possess yourself with love as a friend would
>never pretend not to know what is good
>what you hear today was known millions of years ago
>listen with both ears while your tongue is silent
>those who were your ancestors fell in the stars before
>come to the hour of your ascension
>know that you had an old home before this one shining in the sky over your heads full of wonders not the shadowy existence so many make witness of
>place your hand in theirs when they return and know peace

And
the Hiders of these things did so for thousands of years. Too many men who came to rulership spoke half-truths and if they had known of these things would have become more than the moon itself. Making themselves Gods descended from the Sun and other lies. Pretending that never did men live anywhere else other than here. That men of earth were the sole possessors not only of this galaxy but all galaxies. That science said there are no other witnesses or speakers of intelligence because of carbon, oxygen, and nitrogen and other elements needed for intelligent life to exist. On what other world have they seen trees or water or heard music rise from into space where it could be heard. We have the one that is returning to save mankind after it has been ravaged by an evil one. Who can challenge our holy books and our science?

Atoms know what it means to be wise.

And
because none spoke, the words of these sages spoke louder than all other voices. The people subdued into silence and ignorance of the Book of Books, of ancient galaxies and worlds, of ancestors that brought life to many galaxies and worlds, that travel through time and made witness of the failures and triumphs of ancient civilizations that had ceased to exist now could not ever have existed at all. It is not possible for man to have existed before in other places and knew of good and evil not of this world. Life cannot be billions of years old for is not man a new being, a baby in time made by god from the earth and is not his name Adam and her name Eve and the gods that made him placed him in a garden with a walking snake and trees of good and evil and a tree of life? After billions of years man was made new only here not more than than five or six million years ago?

They
have not considered the Book of Books. The evidence abounding in the law of abundance: where one sun exists so does another, somewhere else. All lives in Space, the soil of creation, exceedingly full of seeds sprouting everywhere in Creation; without end. The law of consciousness exists as the doorway to wisdom and may always be discovered to be the same no matter what world you live on. All this because creation loves itself and you. It is light walking on Space that gives us time and it is time that raises the good and the bad, the beginning and the end.

And
what will you do when you have abandoned the body and closed your eyes to this world: open them in another and work on as if nothing had happened at all.

THE LIVING SCRIPTURES

1. My enemy has become my friend.
2. Across hills of deception where we could not see one another we waged war. After many days we met alone, delivering ourselves to a river of cool running water to meet the Morning and Evening Men.
3. Where have they gone, our soldiers asked kneeling, waiting for the orders of war. Letters were received by many wives whose children asked daily, when is father coming home? The ground was silent. The wind no longer was filled with smoke, the smell of dying bodies. The trees stood ragged with stains of blood and instruments of battle protruding from their trunks.
4. They had been called by a dream entering their world, of another place without a sun or moon or stars, just dry flat land and men marching with their eyes closed into the distance where there are no tomorrows.
5. My enemy, my friend.
6. Generations ago our relatives laughed at the same table. Then a stranger came among us. That stranger rode the Horse of Agony. He presented them with the Box of Plenty. How could we know then that both our hands could not go in the box at the same time?
7. For is not each thing in life placed in its space. No two of us can sit in the same chair for the same purpose. Creation's beauty is its seamless separation. There is only the appearance of the individual. So, the idea of the enemy is the same as the friend. By which degree do we hate one another? How warm does the wood become before it starts to burn.
8. While we sit in this remembered condition the Morning and Evening Men appear before us. Who among us will speak first is the thought on the horizon of this gathering?
9. He that proclaimed to be The Living Scripture rose up: follow me, and all of us ascended the mountain to listen to the words of divine order.
10. What is it that men see and where did they get the original understanding of things?
11. I am the Living Scripture and have come to open your eye and give breath to your heart so that you might live in a greater peace. The four hands make forty and four men make eight points of understanding. The forty-eight give rise to the twelve divisions and the sixty of all combinations are the key to human experience. The body has four limbs and the head sits atop the world for all to see.
12. When did men go down and run after one another? Was and is not your own space enough for you to grapple with without adding others to frames of misery?
13. The woman is for peace if the man is for peace. The woman is for peace when the man is for war. The woman is for peace when the man hunts. When has the woman ever been for war?
The Horse of Agony came riding in the air and the box had no sides only the thought of being dimensional.

14. Each
of your hands is full of lines. The lines are the stories of you as well as your ears and the soles of your feet. Seeing is hearing as walking is talking. The speed of living is the time of living. Those men who follow you are your shadows. The clouds overhead reflections of things they have seen on earth below. All that you see is below you and behind you gone into a past that exists in empty plains you have pushed aside. You have taken yourselves to be kings, to act like suns on a throne with generals that act like Moons or Jupiter or Mars or any of the planets. Each in its own orbit behaving both good and bad as suits them as do you.

15. You
have followed me here to my abode. Sitting silent while I reveal to you great sides which you did not know. And yet, those who follow you submit themselves to your will by the sign of your pen, the words from your mouths, and the pointing of your baby finger. The smallest finger on your hand pointed back at you because these desires of yours are at your whim and your peril. The generations of families that fought against one another sought vengeance for the loss of uncles and brothers and friends.

16. And
in times of peace when the woman could be heard Morning Men rose into prominence. The songs of love and the poetry of sight shone until light fell. Morning Men traveled the earth and the mind. They wanted the rocks and soil and heavens to speak and so they listened for many days to gain understanding. As the nation prospered a neighbor fell grew less and felt as a stepchild feels.

17. The
times emerged for the coming of the Evening Men and all that they knew was theirs. The touching of tree limbs or fields, the pathway of a certain river and an island between them, a tribal marriage all reasons to chip away the skin of a family member and separate. The needlework of the Evening Men designing fabric that was no longer meant to join the two pieces together. Angrily binding up their nation as independent and equal to any who come to their land.

18. I,
The Living Scripture say to you both look and see your own shadows, The Morning and Evening Men. They are not you but walk beside you, in front of you, and behind you. They appear always in their dark form no matter how much light there is. If I were not alive then you could not witness me. I am the living substance of life, the single space of all things outside of me. It is there also where you reside. In this Creation I inhabit you never find a shadow. I walk not upon the ground and I do not fly in the air. I cannot exist without a man or a woman to know of me. I have no eyes or body of any type. I am experience and I only exist because you do.

19. Now,
that you become my witnesses go back to the people as their prophet. One will follow after the other for only one of you can occupy the seat of revelation at a time. And when one of you has passed from this life the other must assume the duty of revelation. And after that has passed from this life then there will be many days before I will make myself known again. It is the cycle of life until mankind rises into the heaven in his mind, each and every one.

20. The Living Scripture
is the most sacred of signs. The teachers from millions of years ago saw this in the living book for men to seek under the Tree of Life. It glimmers as brightly as it did when first known and was already ancient to the most ancient of men. There are other branches of this same light still waiting for a son or daughter to come upon it and gather in the riches of what is hiding under its belly. Spiritual knowledge for refugees weary from the search feed hungrily and sip the sweet water of satisfaction upon discovering that what they saw in a vision was truly real.

21. They
both came down from the mountain they had ascended. Men so full of light and newfound wisdom

that they appeared to be one person in the distance. The soldiers from the nations came to attention marveling at the sight. The two men joined the soldiers and spoke these words:

22. We have all been on a great journey in time. We have fought on the plains of Agony and spilled the blood of ancestors and ourselves. We have cities and lands in ruins, the idea to destroy that which we thought we hated. My heart now surrenders as does my enemy who is now my friend. There was never a war between us only the appearance of separation. We speak the language of love, of children from different nations playing in the waters of life together.

23. If we come upon one another at sea and wave then it is two ships going home after a day's work. What man fishes in the water for another man? What is the bait, alive or dead, that can hook another man? A woman is the bait for a civilized man. The raising of children and the voice of nature suggesting we look here for her secrets.

24. This man here, whose light shines like mine, is my soldier and I am his. We are the army of us and none can stand between us. The space between us exists so that we remain out of each other way. Anything that gets to close to any Sun burns.

25. We have the land to grow on and breath the same air. Let us clear all these battle fields and go home to our wives and children. I hear them calling for us. They are certainly as tired as we are. The war of the human is to be The Living Scripture and greet the Morning Men and chase away the Evening Men wherever they are found to be causing mischief.

peace and peace and peace

ARC OF CREATION

Give
me your eyes to see the Arc of Creation. Cyclones race on planets alive or dead. From whose mouth does this wind come? Religions speak as if they were the words of some god that created only them and only to that god should man bow his head and follow the ordinances announced in a book delivered by the hand of man. These are the Books of Limits. Their orbit cannot go beyond the dominion where they were born and all, in time, go into dissolution. These are the books of warriors that will not allow your eyes to look about to other realms.

Behold
no man can fly into the sky corporeally and transcend from there into heaven to sit on the right side of his father. Heaven is not above only space. There is no heaven beyond the clouds and no man can reappear here again thousands of years later as he was before. Each plant that awakens in spring is not the same plant for the world itself has changed and is not the same. Even the bears of hibernation are different and so is man after a night's sleep. All of this creation is moving toward its day of becoming until it is no longer alive in this creation. The child cannot stay a child forever, nor can the oceans contain themselves not even the stars can remain but one day must go away only to be replaced by others spawning in galactic fields greeted by men seeing their brilliance and little by little becoming witnesses of wisdom their ancestors passed down through millions of generations.

The
Arc of Creation is not a straight line. The winds that spin move in a Arc defying man to track the time of its return to the point of its beginning turn. Easy to see the planets and track their motions; even galaxies have their time. The wise know that returning to the point of origin is different because the entire body and all that it contains is older and wiser because of the many events of gains and losses. What eye does man use to see one point from another and know its hours of spinning? The wind skips over the soil of space, picks up dust and other debris makes deposits on an infinite journey. The seeds of creation are gathered from the destruction of planets and suns making the sound of music as spring dawns in the heavens according to the dispensation of worlds formed under suns. This discourse of the Arc of Creation making worlds words, the language of living bodies seeing themselves and others.

The
eye of men has been betrayed by the words planted in their minds from the Books of Limits. They have men scouring the earth for relics to prove their existence against any thought that wise men can be found elsewhere. Representing themselves as the only answers written thousands of years ago. Do men think the stars they look upon are the same stars from a billion years ago or that men were alive five billion years ago? What is religion but one man's concept of a god that appears like a human? Limiting gods to this world and no other? Make limitless have limits defined by theories and beliefs. Having sixteen children to act as a savior born every six hundred years when the arc of motion reaches a apex in the southern sky. The star of wonder born December 25 in many ancient cultures. If the eyes of a man blinked once perhaps the trance can be broken. Ending the long nightmare of fables and myths of corporeal gods and goddess sitting on thrones replacing the sun and moon. How is it possible for god to have a face or hind parts walking the earth like a man, going to war and poisoning water? Living here instead of everywhere without a body or a name unless men makeup one.

Creation
runs at a speed unimaginable to the wise men of science, philosophy, and religious faith. They all must bend to time one day and time is an arc that bends the whole of all we can see in different

directions. Each spinning in orbits of families of galaxies. Launched billions or trillions of years ago to fulfil all the days of their lives and all the beings of wisdom raised from the farms planted there. And when man takes his instruments and measures the Arc of Creation he will discover the minutest movement creeping through the starry skies. The Arc of Creation bringing the wind to herd and bark its commands against wandering from the path all have set upon. And for all the non-believers look to the fields of the birth of new suns and see the motions of the suns in that galaxy. Eye the direction the wind has pushed it and watch all fall in line as they began their journey slipping noisily across the waters of space. See if its speed is different from all other galaxies near its beginnings. It is a new foal in creation wobbly at first but soon gathering its legs and flying like everybody else.

The
Law of Abundance speaks of the material of creation being plentiful without end. For each sun or galaxy that dissolves many have already been born to add to the family. Gathered by the wind, spun by the wind, until the fire begins and the heavens sparkle full of sunfire born only this morning, even some late at night as we count time. There has never been a time when only one of anything existed. Creation makes and remakes forms without end. It never ceases to move or fall through space.

Blink mankind. Blink and see what you can see now that your eyes have been opened.

Speak
also of colors. The sunfire color is the motion of the vortex spinning in creation. It is the resistance against the wind. What life can there be without friction, without the rub. Light is the gathering of many gases spinning slower than the wind pushing them. Space wind runs wild like rapids. The currents of space wind flow like deep ocean currents. Those that travel in the face of space guide their ships and fly from one world to the next like a ship with sails. Skip from one vortex to the next follow the colors of sunfire lessens the resistance of the eternal winds. Streams of color are winds pouring shade.

Sitting
in wisdom Abundance awaits the followers of the Books of Limits. Trees of plenty drift through scenes of ancient worlds carrying the seeds of revelation with words to make machines only thought possible in dreams. Machines of man copies of the engines that make creation possible. The original last forever and a day. That which man makes soon must be made again better than before.

No
matter how long man pursues the Creation it will always be old the day man understands he knows what he did not know before.

Hzal Anubewei
(Anthony Fudge) was born in Cleveland, Ohio and currently resides in Lithonia, GA. He is an original member of the Muntu Poets formed in 1968. He is the founder of THE OAR Theatrical company, Wrote and produced 2 plays: Migration (Humanist Theater -1973 and They Sing Songs About This performed at Cleveland State, Alleghany State and Second Story Theater (1976-78). He was a co-founder of Black Ascensions Magazine at Tri-c Metro College in Cleveland (1971-72). He has performed original works at Karamu, He was at Albany State College (writer-in-residence '1977), Read at Cleveland State, Howard University, WKYC TV, and radio stations WABQ in Cleveland and WRFG in Atlanta. His works have been published in over 10 anthologies including Freelance; Cleveland Area Arts Council Anthology; The Muntu Poets Anthology 47 Years later; Too Much Boogie in the Blues to name some. He counts among his closest friends and admirers Norman Jordan, Russell Atkins, Owen Dodson, Robert Fleming and Art Nixon. Owen Dodson called him "a word magician". He has read with some of the best-known poets in America including :Amira Baraka, Nikki Giovanni, Quincy Troup, Eugene Redmond, Askia Toure and in a project at Case Western Gwendolyn Brooks identified him in a Call & Post article (1973) as a gifted writer. Hzal has several works of poetry published among them; Migration (1972), The Cry of Beauty (1975), "Diary: The Genius of Love (2000), and Pouring Shade 2018 A Scheme in Every Scene 2015/republished 2020 by Oetryhouse (short stories) The Dead Woman's Bed and Studney and Kilapot a mystery (2021)